CORE CATHARSIS USING PERSONAL MEMES

A New And Radical Approach For Resolving Anxiety, Fully Accepting All Your Experience, And ~~Controlling~~ Engaging Impulses

Lloyd Gregg

www.corecatharsis.com

CONTENTS

ACKNOWLEDGMENTS

I want to thank Judy Schiller and Frank Wall for their input and generous support. Their efforts made this book much more understandable and accessible.

Thanks to Randy Burgess for applying his editing skills and judgment to my scribbles, making them more clear, and turning them into much more of what I meant to say.

I am especially grateful to the many mentors in my life. Without them, this book wouldn't exist.

INTRODUCTION

IN GENERAL

Core Catharsis unites the body with the mind and resolves internal conflict. Impulses and ideas work together for any goal or purpose. Emotions are fully accepted, joined with the thinking mind, and joined with the visceral and somatic senses. Core Catharsis brings self acceptance to a higher and higher level. Positive thinking is transcended to positive experiencing.

Core Catharsis uses simple techniques that fully activate the mind. By using the full mind, ingrained response habits and thought patterns can change quickly. You can quickly transform bad habits into habits you want simply by asking yourself questions. Whether you're aware of it or not, you ask and answer questions almost constantly, and on many different levels. Some types of questions will create fear, insecurity, or repression. Others will create confidence and a sense of feeling comfortable in your own skin. Core Catharsis is about finding and using the right questions.

MORE SPECIFICALLY

Habitual responses are typically created by trauma, excitement, or curiosity. All of these use and activate many faculties of the mind. During a traumatic or exciting experience, most, if not all parts of your mind activate near or at their full capabilities. A dog attack could create an habitual fear response toward all dogs that lasts the rest of your life, even if the attack only lasts three seconds. The excitement of a new romance can create overwhelming joy that you will never forget. In both cases, your mind and body become highly alert and active.

Neuronal Patterns

When you experience anything, neurons activate in your brain. Using synapses, one neuron will transmit a signal to a second neuron, the second to a third, and so on. Repeated experience, or experience that fully activates the mind and body, strengthens neuronal firing patterns in the brain and creates habits.

Examples: Pizza, a First Date, and a Dog

Let's say one thousand neurons activated while Jim ate pizza for lunch. Those neurons gave Jim his sense of taste, smell, feeling the pizza in his hands, and enjoying it. In addition, Jim's experience included warm feelings from his childhood whether he was aware of them or not. On occasion, his father would get pizza for the family as a special treat.

When Jim was fourteen, he asked Jackie to go to a dance and she accepted. Jim liked Jackie very much. He felt extremely nervous and excited at the same time. He worried he might say something stupid or act awkward. He felt excitement with the prospect that Jackie might become his girlfriend.

On their date, Jackie wanted to dance but Jim was too shy. He finally danced with Jackie for the last dance. It was a slow song so Jackie put her arms around him. Jim was going through puberty. He had strong feelings he never had before. When Jim took Jackie to her home, she kissed and hugged him for five minutes before she went inside.

If Jim had one thousand neurons activate while having pizza, probably five million activated about his date with Jackie. So, it wouldn't be surprising if Jim couldn't remember having pizza for lunch, but he'll remember his date with Jackie for the rest of his life and in great detail. Jim's experience gave him a strong sense of how wonderful a romance can be. This sense stayed with him and affected all of his relationships.

3

Imagine the effect on Jim if Jackie spent the evening with another guy because Jim didn't want to dance at first.

When Jim was four years old, a dog attacked him. Jim's mind and body became highly activated. He experienced the fight-or-flight response. His heart pounded long after he was safe in his home. He wouldn't go outside for three days for fear he would encounter the dog, even though his parents told him the neighbors sent the dog to a farm. Many neurons fired in his brain during the attack and long after the attack. Even though the attack only lasted three seconds, Jim developed a strong automatic fear response that overwhelmed him whenever he saw a dog.

So, trauma and excitement activate the mind and body. Both can be a very effective ways to create response habits. Trauma is certainly not a desirable way. Jim would rather not be afraid of all dogs. Excitement isn't practical. You only get one first date, and Jim's date could have been terrible if Jackie left him for another boy. That leaves curiosity. By using questions, we can be curious about anything we experience, and build any habit we want.

QUESTIONS

Questions activate many parts of the mind. Questions fire neurons and create strong pathways in the brain that create strong memories, habits, and automatic responses. This is how you have created most, if not all, of your current spontaneous habits and responses. You probably didn't mean to create your habits. You probably weren't aware you were creating them. Fear, anger, trauma, and anxiety naturally use questions even if there is no conscious question you ask yourself. When Jim was attacked by a dog, he didn't consciously ask himself anything. His mind, and body, became highly activated and implicitly asked--WHAT DO I DO NOW? From this activation, his mind created several strong response habits whether he wanted them or not.

You already create habits by asking yourself questions. However, the types of questions you use might not give you the results you want.

Compare these two questions
- How do I stop feeling like a loser?
- How can my feeling like a loser help me to achieve anything I want?

The mind is like a computer. It will look for answers to either question. It doesn't care if you're a loser or not, or if the question makes sense. The longer you ask either question, the more you'll activate neurons in many parts of your brain. You'll get more and more answers. More importantly, you'll start to develop a habit of looking for answers to the question you choose.

The first question, "How do I stop feeling like a loser?" will lead toward repressing your feelings and ever more anxiety. The second question includes your feelings in the task of accomplishing what you want. By including your feelings, you don't create internal conflict. Feelings become comfortable from focusing attention on them, and seeing them as part of you and your goals.

Imagine life without conflict between your thoughts and feelings. No matter what you feel, you automatically find how that feeling can help with anything you're trying to accomplish, or with people you're trying to love. It's never necessary to spend energy trying to repress a feeling or a thought.

How can that be possible? Because the mind is completely pliable. It will look for answers to any question, even these:
- How can hate help me love?
- How can my pain help create pleasure?
- How does $2 + 2 = 5$?

If you don't care that a question makes sense or not, your mind won't either. We already ask questions like, why am I such a loser? If you think about it, that's a silly question, but we ask questions like that frequently.

So, Core Catharsis is about asking better questions--
questions that inherently unite your thoughts and feelings:

- How can my feelings help me with anything I'm doing?
- How can my anger with so and so, help me better connect with them?

HOWEVER, Core Catharsis is NOT about answers (although, uniting thoughts and feelings frequently creates great insight). Core Catharsis is about metamorphosis. Questions can create a metamorphosis with conflicted thoughts and feelings. The very same thoughts and feelings that cause turmoil can be repurposed or reconfigured. Nothing of what you already are needs to be repressed or discarded. The purpose of the questions is to build neuronal pathways you want--that is, habits and personal memes you want ("personal memes" is described later in the book.)

While asking questions, most of the activity in your mind doesn't come to your awareness. Your mind churns away looking for answers, but you only notice the answers and insights that seem significant to you. Those answers are only pieces of the entire process or journey. Without taking the entire journey, the same insights would seem meaningless to you. That's why an idea you come up with on your own can feel like a powerful revelation. When someone else tells you the same idea, you barely notice. The journey, or search, builds the mental connections you need, not the answers or insights. For building existential comfort, to question is the answer.

Here's a personal example. I've always had a tendency to feel dejected. At times, I'll feel inferior to everyone as if they have more power and more confidence. I began to look for and find how those feelings could help me. I activated my full mind by asking myself, over and over, how my feelings of dejection can help me.

From doing that, I realized that people might ignore me for many reasons. I realized that my need to feel heard or appreciated won't always match another person's mood.

6

They might feel the same need at the same time or have other things on their mind.

I began to feel comfortable with those feelings. Before, I would fight or ignore them. The same feelings that were painful now help me. Those same feelings now remind me that I'm not feeling as connected to others as I want. Then, depending on what I sense in others, I can ask for what I want, decide to be compassionate, let them alone until they're in a better mood, or not try to be their friend at all.

However, my comfort didn't come from those realizations or insights. It came from activating my full mind with the question of how my feelings can help me. Insights were just by-products of that process. Since I asked how my current feelings can help, there was no repression. I didn't need to ignore anything I already am, or try to break a habit.

That is how Core Catharsis is different from most other approaches. Understanding emotions is not the primary goal. The goal is to build emotions and responses you want, using what you already are.

HOW TO USE THIS BOOK

Whenever a technique uses a question, it will be
emboldened and preceded with a question mark like this:
? How can these feelings help me with _____?

The techniques are mostly separate from the explanations of
the techniques. The techniques begin on page 28, and end
on page 126. The rest of the book explains the techniques.

The best way to use this book depends how you like to
teach yourself anything. If you'd rather learn by doing, then
you might not need to read the explanation sections very
much. If you want to learn by doing, first practice the Ten
Answers Technique, page 28.

You'll at least need to read the section describing personal
memes starting on page 10. It's a concept that's particular
to this book and it's used throughout the book. Other than
that, it's probably a matter of practicing the techniques and
reading the explanation sections as needed.

The explanations are important in the same way they're
important with explaining how to play basketball, or the
piano. Explanations can help you practice in better ways.
They can encourage you to practice, but skill only develops
with practice. Knowing everything there is to know about
basketball, or the piano, won't make you more skilled at
either.

On page 44 (A SUGGESTION), the book changes focus a
little. Until then, the techniques use the thinking mind
(usually with questions) to direct attention toward feelings
and bodily sensations. After that section, the techniques
assume you can focus attention on bodily sensations directly
without using a question or thought.

That does NOT mean being able to focus attention on
sensations directly is better or more advanced than using

questions. I can directly focus on sensations only on rare occasions, like when I'm tired or depressed.

This book is mostly structured this way because sections later in the book are older. Those sections didn't use questions originally.

UNDERSTANDING THE TECHNIQUES

PERSONAL MEMES

To effectively describe Core Catharsis, I'm using the word "meme" differently then its current usage. I'm applying its characteristics to a single mind instead of many minds. The word "meme" has similar characteristics as the word "gene." In one region of the world, most people will have brown hair, and in other regions most people will have black or blonde hair. Red hair is a genetic trait, but it's not as common as black, brown, or blonde hair. These are characteristics of genes.

The current definition of the word meme (introduced by Richard Dawkins), has similar characteristics as genes. It refers to cultural tastes like music, fashion, or political beliefs. Think of all the minds of the world as parts of one mind--a mass mind. This mass mind has many memes, and some are stronger or more pervasive than others. The Beatles became a strong pervasive meme in a fairly short period of time. 911 (nine eleven), Pearl Harbor, and JFK are examples of memes that became very strong almost instantly. Many, if not most, of the people in the world could have much to say upon simply hearing 911.

Other memes are weak. I don't remember most of the stories I see on the local news. Unless someone mentions a story the next day, I'll probably forget the story in a few days. However, if a story included an interview with me, it would be a strong meme, but only to me. The story would still be a weak meme to other people who watched the news. For the world, the mass mind, it would be a very weak meme since most people didn't see the story.

Why some memes become prominent, and others don't, is frequently mysterious. Advertisers sometimes spend millions of dollars advertising a product, yet it doesn't become popular. Sometimes a product or fashion becomes very popular with little advertising. It's as if the mass mind has preferences or moods just like individual minds.

Memes are also part of Core Catharsis, but instead of applying the characteristics of memes to the mass mind, they are applied to a single mind--your mind. You could think of a meme as a single thought, but Core Catharsis primarily deals with ingrained thought patterns that contain many thoughts or perceptions such as habits, desires, and impulses. Liking strawberries but hating cantaloupe are both personal memes. The fear of snakes is a meme. Ingrained pleasurable responses are memes as well as ingrained responses of discomfort. Moods, cravings, anxiety, fear, anger, shyness, introversion, and extroversion are all memes. Your personality is the sum total of all of your memes.

Like cultural memes, your personal memes can be strong or weak for mysterious reasons. A song might play in your mind for no apparent reason. Someone could love to play golf, even though they don't play well. Sometimes, we're strongly attracted to people we have nothing in common with.

Memes usually don't change quickly and usually follow consistent patterns. If you're an introvert, you're almost always an introvert. Your likes and dislikes don't change much from one day to the next. Habits seem hard to break. If you don't like the taste of cantaloupe, telling yourself that you've changed your mind wouldn't make it taste good.

Like genes, memes change over time. Most teenagers feel very hurt when someone makes fun of them. Most thirty year olds barely notice when someone makes fun of them. If you got an opportunity to become rich by being a snake handler, you'd at least think about changing your fear of snakes meme.

Unlike genes, personal memes can sometimes change instantly. We can hate someone for years, have a big fight with them, and then be best friends. All those years of hatred suddenly turn into friendship. The fight somehow caused a catharsis. There was no need to spend months trying to break the habit of hating that particular person. That habit just goes away. The meme changes dramatically on its own--somehow.

Curiosity develops memes. Curiosity develops complex skills that become automatic. You engaged most of your mind, and bodily sensations, when you wondered how to stay balanced on a bicycle. Soon, you could ride anywhere you wanted to go.

You've made numerous mental connections and associations with letters of the alphabet to form words and words to form sentences. Now you have a very complex meme that can understand anything another person writes. Just as you've used curiosity to learn, you can use it to change your spontaneous reactions to anxiety and stress.

Blocking Memes, Bob, and a Bear

The following is an example of how a blocking meme can develop. While Bob watches television in his living room, a bear walks in, looks around, and leaves without attacking him. That was more than enough to traumatize Bob. Since he had no way to leave the room or fight the bear, his mind went into fright mode as a way to protect him from overwhelming fear. Bob's fright also prepared him to become unconscious so he could painlessly experience being eaten by the bear, even though that didn't happen.

Bob lost his ability to notice details. His attention became frozen. If someone asked him to count the number of toes on the bear, he wouldn't be able to. In a zoo, counting a bear's toes would be extremely easy.

Because of his trauma, he can no longer go into his living room or even walk by it. He can't afford to move so he has a friend get the things he needs from the room. Now he only stays in his bedroom. Whenever he sees the door to his living room at the end of the hallway, he averts his eyes. Bob will have no new experience with his living room. He will automatically resist anyone's attempt to get him to go into the room. He will automatically resist any attempt by his own mind to think about the room. Bob has developed a blocking meme.

Persistent Memes

A persistent meme is any mental state that is persistent such as: moods, depression, cravings, or a song that keeps playing in your mind. Blocking memes frequently cause persistent memes or cause persistent memes to last longer than they would otherwise. Since blocking memes block awareness, no further understanding or perspective can occur so there is no opportunity for catharsis. Until Bob deals with the blocks about going back into his living room, his fear and avoidance memes will persist. Bob has no access to a perspective that would help him feel comfortable using his living room again.

Moods, depression, and cravings tend to last longer when we fight or block them. Fighting or repressing any experience only causes anxiety. If you indulge a song that keeps playing in your mind, you don't get anxious. If you just let it play, it eventually loses its persistence. Also, when you don't block or fight a meme, you'll be open to any information it might have. You'll be open to the reason it's persisting. Frequently, when I think about the lyrics to a song that's playing in my head, it perfectly fits something that's happening in my life.

Optional Memes

Memories and knowledge are examples of optional memes. The memory of my third grade teacher doesn't persistently come into my awareness. I can remember her if I want to. If I don't want to, that memory will easily go back where it came from. I didn't create any blocking or persistent memes

13

from my experience with her. See WORKING WITH HUNGER, page 94.

The techniques of Core Catharsis can be used with any meme. You don't always have to work on anxiety or blocking memes. You can develop and deepen pleasurable experiences. An easy way to start Core Catharsis is to only practice the techniques by using pleasant memories. That can give you a good sense of how the techniques work to build memes and habits you want. Eventually though, you'll naturally want to veer toward memes that include some anxiety. See CATHARSIS AND PLEASURE, page 26.

USING QUESTIONS

If you're looking for something you haven't seen before, you're in question or search mode (see page 25). Learning, analysis, and examination are also forms of questioning. With those, you're at least looking for new perspectives or understandings.

When you look for new understandings or perspectives, your mind will use any or all of its faculties until it finds an answer. It will search all of your databases. It will activate your right and left hemisphere, your cerebrum, cerebellum, limbic system, and so on. You will use any mental faculty you have in any part of your brain until you find an answer. You'll likely search your memories for something similar to your question. You'll connect thoughts and emotions in new ways until you find something that fits what you're looking for. You might use words in different ways, or create visual images arranged in new ways.

But all of that happens subconsciously. An idea only becomes conscious when you sense you've found a suitable or useful answer. If you then decide that answer isn't exactly right, you'll continue the search for a better one.

During all that mental activity, many synapses fire between neurons and pass data from one neuron to the next. They fire in particular patterns best suited to your question. When you sense a pattern that best fits your question, you stop searching. You've found an answer.

If you then use the pattern repeatedly, it becomes ingrained. For example, you look on a map for the best way to drive to a job interview. You memorize the route, or pattern, as best you can. Maybe you make some wrong turns the first time. If you get the job, you drive that route every day. You reinforce that pattern or meme every day. The neural pathways in your mind become stronger. After a couple of weeks, you drive the route without thinking about it.

Let's go back to the trauma caused by the bear walking into Bob's living room, and use questions to affect his blocking memes. Notice I said affect the blocking memes instead of remove the blocking memes. The word remove isn't accurate to describe the process just like it's not accurate to say someone removes their lap when they stand up. In both cases, nothing is removed, purged, or destroyed. There's simply a change of use or viewpoint. (see, WHAT IS CATHARSIS?, page 128, for more)

For Bob, affecting his blocking memes could be as simple as asking himself to remember exactly what happened, and to start looking for and remembering details about the bear. His mind will try to remember anything he asks. However, in this case, the first and strongest memory about the bear is his painful fear. He experienced fright. The fright response is full of fear, pain, and an inability to look for details. Bob doesn't want to remember and experience fear and pain again. That's part of the reason he created a blocking meme.

Answers Aren't the Goal of Asking Questions

Bob decides he wants to go back into his living room but he knows he can't deal with experiencing his fear. He asks himself, how can I feel comfortable going into my living room? He asks himself how his fear can help him feel comfortable. Of course, his first answer is, how the heck would I know? However, Bob read this book about six months ago and has been practicing the techniques. He knows that looking for answers to these questions will help create comfort.

He asks himself those questions again and again. He thinks maybe he could have a friend go in his living room with him. There are no wild bears within one hundred miles of his home. Bob's bear escaped from a traveling zoo a half mile away. He could make sure there isn't a traveling zoo near him. He could go to a zoo and look at the bears. Bob keeps asking those questions again and again looking for new answers.

At first, none of the answers that came to him included remembering anything about the bear. His mind still avoided doing that. Eventually though, he did remember. He remembered that he noticed a movement in his peripheral vision, turned his head and saw the bear looking at him. The bear raised its snout as if to smell something. Then the bear left. Bob thought, maybe the bear didn't like how he smelled. That thought made him smile. Then Bob felt an incredible release of physical tension. Bob had a catharsis. Bob was ready to go into his living room.

Normally, Bob would have stopped looking for answers after the first or second answer. Going to the zoo and watching bears could have also created a catharsis but he didn't need to do that. By continuing to look for answers, Bob's blocking memes faded away.

The Goal Is to Create Or Update a Meme to the Point of Having a Catharsis.

So, if answers aren't the goal, why all the questions? Understanding the heading of this section is critical to understanding this book and getting something out of it. So, I'll repeat: **The goal is to create or update a meme to the point of having a catharsis.** The more questions asked, the better. Questions activate many areas of the mind. Other memes join in the effort, awareness increases and blockage decreases.

Bob's idea of having a friend with him included many memes about his friends. He has many ideas about his friends and he has many feelings about his friends. Those memes live in several different parts of his mind. Those memes connected to his ideas about how safe his neighborhood is, and how unlikely it would be that another bear would walk into his living room. Those memes connected to his next answer, and so on.

Bob's question was about feeling more comfortable, so that's what his mind tried to answer. His mind found answers in a sequence that was exactly right for Bob. His mind didn't focus on the bear until it had followed all the mental paths it needed to directly think about the bear in a comfortable way.

From experience with the techniques, Bob had realized that fully remembering pain, even for a split second, won't occur until he is ready. His mind will protect itself. It won't bring pain to awareness until all needed mental connections and memes can bring it to awareness in a comfortable way.

At first, Bob's blocking meme, and pain, were as strong as ever. However, his mind now had something to do in addition to blocking his awareness and blocking his pain. It had the task of finding ways to feel comfortable so Bob could use his living room again. Bob's question instantly made his pain and fear allies to his goal. That began to create comfort with the same feelings Bob had been blocking. If Bob's blocking meme and pain returned, the pain would be less. The pain became a reminder to ask his question again, and that would reduce the pain even more.

While searching for answers, the blocking meme was inactive, so Bob experienced his physical reaction without the pain of blocking it. His physical reaction was stress caused by adrenalin and every other way his body reacts to fear. However, that reaction isn't different from what he would feel if he parachuted from an airplane. In that case, he wouldn't block his fear, and he might enjoy it.

So, each time Bob asks his question, his pain reduces. He realizes, more and more, that his physical reaction isn't overwhelming or something he needs to block. Each time he asks his question, he builds a meme along side his blocking meme. When his new meme is strong enough, or as strong as the blocking me, the blocking meme will have lost its persistence. Since the new meme is comfortable, he will naturally pick it over the blocking meme.

A Tipping Point

The more Bob asked questions about being comfortable, the stronger his new memes became. At a point, a tipping point, the new meme's power at least equaled the power of his blocking meme. Both became options and Bob could choose either one. Of course, he chose the one that wasn't painful.

Catharsis can be thought of as a new balance, association, or both, between two or more memes. When Bob had his catharsis, he didn't destroy his blocking meme. It became an option. If the memory of the bear pops into his mind while he's reading a book, he can choose to think about the memory or go back to reading his book. He can willfully "block" the memory of the bear. However, the word block is no longer an accurate description for what he's doing since he is simply choosing between two options. Since Bob has a clear option, he naturally remembers the bear without feeling the pain and fear he felt before he had an option. He could try to experience that pain again, but it would be difficult since he has an option. Much of his pain was caused by not having an option.

Pliability of Mind

If you don't care that a question you ask yourself makes sense or not, your mind won't either. Your mind is pliable or flexible. It will work on anything you ask of it. To test this, I asked myself how $2 + 2 = 5$. I put aside the idea the question is crazy and sincerely looked for answers. My first three answers were, 2 + 2 doesn't equal 5. Than it occurred to me, 2 + 2 = 4 + me. I'm part of the equation. There are five elements to the equation. Without me, would there be an equation? That has meaning to me if only on a philosophical level, or it's just a fun way to look at it. I'm sure, if you try, your mind would come up with a different answer that has meaning to you, whether the answer is crazy or not.

Let's look at a more practical example. Jon is very angry with his wife, Marcy. He keeps asking himself how he married such a jerk. How was he so stupid? His mind dutifully looks for answers to those questions whether Jon is aware of it or not. With those questions, what memes would he create? What's more likely for Jon, divorce or a happy marriage?

Instead, Jon asks how his anger can help him get along with Marcy. He uses the pliability of his mind. That is, he puts aside the idea that the question doesn't make sense and tries anyway. His mind dutifully looks for answers because it doesn't care if the question makes sense or not. Even though Jon has never thought anger could be helpful in any way, his mind looks for how it could be. The mind is pliable, or flexible, in the same way a dog will fetch any stick. The dog doesn't care what it's made from or even if it's too big. Bob will get all kinds of answers. Some will be rational, some will be wildly irrational, but Jon is trying to build a useful meme, not find reasonable answers to his problem.

By using that question, Jon's feelings and thoughts would work toward the same goal. His internal world would become united--not conflicted and uncomfortable. He wouldn't reinforce or develop the negative ideas that he is stupid or Marcy is a jerk. The question is inherently accepting of his anger and of Marcy. As Jon's blocking memes fade away, he would likely begin to understand what his anger is about. Maybe if he could get Marcy to stop interrupting him, he would feel more connected to her--or maybe this or that.

The more he asks his question, the more he will develop a natural sense of curiosity about his anger and his wife. Marcy, consciously or not, will feel accepted when Jon approaches her with a natural sense of curiosity. When he tells her he doesn't like when she interrupts him, she'll more likely hear him. If he approaches her with a sense that she's a jerk, he'll likely hear Marcy angrily tell him how he is a bigger jerk. This is an example of how the techniques of Core Catharsis use pliability of mind in a beneficial way. The next time Jon feels anger toward Marcy, the option to look for how his anger can help him will be available. That meme will become stronger and stronger the more he uses it.

Generalization and Begging the Question.

Most of the questions are general so you can add your personal details. Let's look at this question, how can I feel more comfortable loving people more? That question inherently "begs" for more concrete details. What exactly is more comfortable and what is loving? If you sincerely look for new answers to that question, your mind will add the concrete details of what those words mean to you. It will likely use many parts of your mind and mental faculties. You'll develop a meme that contains specific concrete actions, even if those actions never come to your conscious mind.

Picking a question that's too general or too specific is always a concern. Sometimes, a general question might feel right one day but not the next. One day you might favor a general question like, how can I feel more comfortable loving everyone more? The next day you might prefer something more specific like, how can I feel more comfortable loving _____ (a specific person) more? With practice, you'll get a better sense of when a question is too general or too specific.

FOCUSING ATTENTION ON FEELINGS AND BODILY SENSATIONS

The ability to focus on bodily sensations is a key part of Core Catharsis. The techniques almost always include a reference to feelings or bodily sensations. For example, how can these feelings help me to _____?

Feeling more comfortable, and eliminating pointless anxiety, are some of the objectives of this book. Most of the questions also include a goal, usually the goal of feeling better. The questions are usually structured to be inclusive and integrative. That is, they promote all parts of the mind working together and for the same goal. They don't promote internal conflict. One way you can be sure you're using the questions correctly (if there is such a thing), is to try to get at least three new ideas, perspectives, or feelings about the subject of your question.

Without including your bodily sensations, it's possible to create new mental or emotional perspectives, and still feel as anxious and uncomfortable as ever. Bodily sensations from memes created by trauma, excitement, or anxiety, don't necessarily change just because you have a better understanding of them. You can clearly see every aspect of an issue, but still have a habit, or meme, of feeling anxious about it.

You could fully understand everything about public speaking, but still feel uncomfortable doing it. Someone else could learn how to use the excitement and increased adrenaline that come with public speaking to help them give a great speech. They wouldn't need to analyze every aspect of public speaking. They simply connect their goals to their nervous feelings and find ways to use them. That creates a comfortable meme. They no longer experience their feelings as nervous fear; they experience it as excitement.

When a question includes a reference to bodily sensations or feelings, it directs attention toward them. That attention causes relaxation of muscles and nerves that don't need to be tense. How tense are the muscles around your eyes right now? By asking that question once, those muscles probably started to relax rather you tried to relax them or not. Ask it for twenty minutes and those muscles, and much of your body, will become very relaxed. Any part of the body immediately responds to attention like people respond to compliments. Your body likes attention. It doesn't take effort to relax muscle tension. Simply focusing attention on bodily sensations relaxes muscle tension naturally.

Bob's questions were primarily about his body. Bob's issue was feeling uncomfortable. Asking questions that referenced his feelings addressed that discomfort. A question that didn't reference his feelings wouldn't address his core issue. His discomfort blocked his ability to think about his experience with the bear. As soon as he started to feel comfortable, the blocks to his thinking mind naturally faded away.

Imagine if Bob asked, how do I get rid of this fear about the bear? What type of meme would that create? Fear at least indirectly refers to feelings or bodily sensations, so that question would block Bob's bodily sensations. It promotes internal conflict by blocking the feelings of fear. It doesn't refer to feeling comfortable, so Bob's tension might never go away. He could easily create a meme that ignores his tension or pretends it's not there. He could sit in his living room but with a constant underlying anxiety that drains his energy.

CATHARSIS

Catharsis is the point, the tipping point, when a new meme becomes as strong as a blocking meme. The blocking meme becomes an option when it wasn't before.

You could also think of catharsis as a metamorphosis of emotion, like when a caterpillar becomes a butterfly. When attention is directed toward bodily sensations and emotions, it causes them to bloom or move toward their next stage of development. Anger becomes drive or ambition. Hatred becomes empathy or understanding. Depression becomes rest, or needed clarity about overwhelming circumstances.

Now that Bob's blocks are optional, he can apply the full power of his awareness and skills to create even more options. With his new options, he can enter his living room. He doesn't need to further understand his fear about the bear to feel comfortable in his living room. However, he wanted to understand more, and now he can freely focus on any part of his previously blocked experience. He remembered as much as he could about the bear. He thought about finding the traveling zoo and getting a good look at the bear. Bob felt sympathy for the bear. After the bear left Bob, the police chased it up a tree and shot it with a tranquilizer gun. The poor bear must have been afraid.

If a new meme contains physical relaxation and it becomes as strong as a blocking meme, the mind will naturally favor the new meme. Bob's fear and pain didn't go away and he didn't fight either one. His fear and pain were no longer mandatory or the only options. At the tipping point, he naturally selected the comfortable option. At that point, it seemed that his physical tension, pain, and fear suddenly relaxed and released. Bob experienced a catharsis. For Bob, it was one of the most exciting and pleasurable experiences of his life.

Feeling a sudden relaxation of physical tension is common when practicing Core Catharsis. The techniques can remove resistance very quickly and you can do it anytime you want. You've probably already used the techniques of Core Catharsis many times just by happenstance. For example, we can develop strong hatred (resistance) toward another person that lasts for years based on a mistaken idea that they somehow wronged us. This frequently happens in family relationships. When we suddenly discover we weren't wronged, or they in no way meant to wrong us, we might feel disoriented or even shocked from the sudden shift in perspective. We will also feel great relief or catharsis. The hatred (resistance), and years of tension toward that person are suddenly gone. The ingrained perspective that included resistance is suddenly invalid. The mind works frantically and many synapses fire between neurons in the brain to create connections that don't include resistance. We quickly establish a new or altered meme about the family member. With Core Catharsis, you can create new memes anytime you want. You don't have to wait for happenstance or circumstances to create better memes and physical comfort.

The previous example involves a sudden change in a belief. Much of our core life long anxieties are based in sensory perception, not belief. Ingrained fear, anger, anxiety, and the associated blocking memes, can develop in early childhood before we have language or the ability to believe in any idea. Since the techniques of Core Catharsis are based on building memes, achieving a catharsis with early childhood anxieties is as easy as catharsis with anxieties based on a belief. In both cases, a new meme develops that accepts the feelings of the anxiety. When that acceptance is equally powerful to a blocking meme, the block becomes an option. Sensory perception is no longer blocked.

However, working with early childhood anxiety can seem difficult at first. The thinking mind and its beliefs can easily get in the way of catharsis with these anxieties. Early childhood anxieties developed primarily from sensory perception, that is, our five (probably more) senses. We didn't describe those anxieties with an idea or mental handle because we didn't have that ability. That's the primary reason that trying to understand these feelings, or assigning a definition to them, has little effect. Frequently, it further represses them:
- We might think we have a feeling figured out so we stop focusing attention on it.
- We have an insight or revelation that feels great, but that insight doesn't build a significant meme. It only stops further exploration of the feeling.

We soon forget the insight and the automatic nature of our original feelings causes them to return. Then we try to figure them out again, have another wonderful insight, forget that insight, and on and on. Perhaps over months or years, that process builds a strong meme that adds an option to the blocking meme. With Core Catharsis, you don't have to spend that much time. You can quickly build a meme that includes comfortable feelings and any other element you want, not just ideas.

Catharsis with childhood anxieties can also be difficult because those anxieties are so familiar. We strongly identify with them. We're attached to them. Even though they might be painful, we're afraid we wouldn't be ourselves if we resolved those blocking memes and turned them into options. With practice, you'll see there's really nothing to fear.

THE MIND'S SEARCH MODE

Search mode is simply whatever your mind does when you ask yourself a question. I wish I could define it further but I doubt we'll ever understand it in meaningful detail. I'd be very curious about the brain activity an MRI would show when someone tries to answer a question, especially a question like, how can I feel more comfortable with _____? Would a question like that activate the same area of the brain in the same sequence from one day to the next? How would the patterns change the longer the question is asked and the stronger the memes become?

When you ask yourself a question, your mind searches your experiential databases. Your mind looks here and there. It associates and compares. It puts two or more experiences together that haven't been associated before. Your mind will search as long as you ask questions. You'll use any or all of your faculties. Involving more of your faculties builds stronger optional memes and leads to catharsis.

Questions in Core Catharsis are primarily used to activate search mode. Any answers you get are as important as ever, but they are not a stopping point no matter how profound an answer seems.

Search mode is also part of analysis, inquiry, examination, investigation, wonder, scrutiny, and confusion. Asking ourselves questions is how we can access those. Fear also has an inherent question or search mode. In its basic form, fear only has two answers: fight or run away. That works well--if you're a caveman. In modern life, fear can be continuous in the form of anxiety. Fortunately, the searching mind can create new memes that affect anxiety in a positive way.

Search mode can even be part of a static thought or a dogmatic belief. If you stick to a particular idea, you will need to search for ways to maintain your belief when you sense something doesn't fit with your belief. For example, watch any television show with political pundits arguing their opposing views. Pundit A will search for examples and facts that support their viewpoint no matter how well pundit B shows that pundit A is incorrect.

CATHARSIS AND PLEASURE

This book generally centers on achieving catharsis by focusing on unpleasant habitual experiences. However, focusing on pleasant experience can be dynamic, interesting, and just as cathartic as focusing on resisted experience. No matter what you focus on, you will experience it in more detail. You'll create more memes. Focusing on something that is already pleasurable can make it more pleasurable. Or, you might realize that you've been getting pleasure from others' pain or from something you'd rather not get pleasure.

Here's a personal example of gaining more pleasure from something I already found pleasurable. For several years, I walked to work using the same route through a park. It was always a pleasant part of my day. One day, when I wasn't working, I happened to walk much the same route with my camera. I searched for anything that would make a good picture. That search was much more detailed, and a much different view of what I had looked at hundreds of times before. The next time I walked to work, it was different, more pleasant, and more interesting than ever before.

THE TECHNIQUES

Focused or On The Fly, Which Is The Best Way?

You should work with a question in a focused way. You should sit down in a quiet room, clear your mind, and focus only on your question with as few distractions as possible.

No. Wait. You should just work toward catharsis as you go about your daily life. Only apply the techniques when you feel the need and to the real things and people in your life. That's the natural and organic way to do it.

The answer is: do all of the above or any combination of the two. Working with a question in a diligent and focused way is usually best with memories, habitual emotions, and habits in general. Working on the fly is usually best for dealing with impulses and reactions that you don't like whether they're habitual or not. However, there are many exceptions. Developing a sense of what works best for you is an important part of practicing these techniques.

Working with Questions in a Focused Way with the Ten Answers Technique

The following technique can be used with any question and it can be very powerful. This technique, more than anything else in this book, will show you what Core Catharsis is and how it can dramatically affect your habits and emotions. As a warning, I suggest that you first practice it with something you normally find pleasurable, and then with something that is only slightly upsetting or annoying.

The ten answers technique is:
- Write down at least ten answers to the question you decide to work with. Try the continuous writing technique (page 124) if you feel stuck or overwhelmed.

28

- Rate each answer on how accurate or useful it **feels**. Don't rate it on how accurate or useful you think it is. You can use a rating of 1 to 10: 1 = doesn't feel accurate or useful at all, 10 = feels completely accurate or useful.
- If you feel ten answers aren't enough to create a useful new meme or catharsis, write more answers or review the answers you already have to see if you feel differently about the rating you gave them originally.

For some questions, especially emotionally charged questions, you might need a few days to complete ten answers. For example, it took me several days to complete ten answers with:

? How can my feelings about anger directed toward me, help me to better relate to the angry person?

For me, working with this activated very intense feelings. I needed to take some time to let them settle in. However, I gained much comfort from working with this question. I fully realized, mentally and viscerally, how vulnerable I was to others' anger and that I had options for how I can react to it. I spent a few hours working on the answers and because of that I created a new meme. That meme automatically made me more aware of others' anger and the new options I had for reacting to their anger. I automatically reacted to others' anger by telling them I didn't like it, and at the same time I was sympathetic to their frustration that caused their anger.

Working with Questions On The Fly

Much of your daily experience isn't static like a memory or an ingrained habit. Many impulses are completely about what is happening to you now such as hunger, sexual attraction, tension from dealing with traffic, and so on. For example, sometimes I feel much resistance about going to the gym. From working with that resistance while walking to the gym, I realized that sometimes I was just being lazy, and sometimes I was exhausted and I needed rest more than a workout. Exhaustion usually isn't based in an ingrained habit.

29

However, impulses that are not ingrained habits can have associated impulses that are. I don't think I have many associated impulses about feeling exhausted. I'm sure I have repression, and many associated ingrained habitual impulses with sexual attraction. I might feel it's wrong or become frustrated with having more sexual feelings than I know what to do with.

Working with memes on the fly has the advantage of using your sensory perception to connect or associate comfort with real things in your daily life. Conversely, working with a question in a focused manor mostly uses your imagination. However, the more successful you are with a focused approach, the more it becomes part of your daily experience. If you use your imagination to create a meme about how to deal with angry people, that meme will automatically affect you when you experience angry people--on the fly.

? How much are these feelings based in the past?
Working with this question can help you decide if you want to work on something in a focused way, or an on-the-fly way.
There's no way to know for sure how much an impulse or emotion comes from a past or present experience. Fortunately, the techniques of Core Catharsis are geared toward uniting your feelings with all of your experience. You don't necessarily need to know if your feelings are based in the past or not. However, this question can help you decide the best approach for experiencing any feeling or emotion.

Remember, any answers you get, no matter how insightful, profound, or stupid, are not a stopping point. The goal is to build comfortable memes and achieve catharsis. The goal is better memes, NOT answers. All answers, stupid or profound, are just a side effect or by-product of asking a question over and over.

THE BASIC OR MOST USED TECHNIQUES OR QUESTIONS

Practicing the techniques in this section should give you basic tools and skills for engaging all aspects of your life. The questions cover most personal and social discomfort caused by blocking memes. You might want to memorize the questions you're working on, or make a list you can carry with you. These are example questions. With a little practice, you'll likely start wording them differently to better address your experience.

As much as possible, the questions follow this basic format: How can my <u>current feelings</u> help me to <u>feel better</u> and <u>achieve a goal</u>.

Interaction With Others

These questions address the basic aspects of interacting with others. They help create useful memes with feeling rejected or disrespected, feeling controlled, miscommunication, jealousy, shyness, fear, aggression, selfishness, or empathy.

These questions might seem particularly odd. As always, they're for building memes that unite all parts of your mind and resolve internal conflict. Getting answers to these questions isn't the primary goal. However, you might be surprised at how well your mind can come up with rational answers to a question like, how can my hatred of someone help me love them? See, Pliability of Mind, page 18.

Fear and Anger

? How can my feelings about anger directed toward me, help me with someone who is angry with me?
? How can my feelings about someone who fears me help me relate to them?
This last question can create a powerful revelation. We can be oblivious to the fear someone feels about us since we're so wrapped up with our own pain. This question can create

31

empathy for others when they feel fear about our actions, even if we don't mean to cause fear and even if their reaction is based in something that has nothing to do with our actions. This question can also create the sobering realization that sometimes we behave badly and cause reasonable fear in others.

? How can my feelings of anger toward someone help me communicate with them?
? How can my feelings of fear of someone help me to feel comfortable with them?

I feel the above four questions cover the basic problems, with relating to anyone--fear and anger. The following questions are more specific, but anger or fear usually play a part with the issues they address.

? How can any of my feelings help me with the social life I want?
This question can be a powerful and effective way to increase your comfort around others. It can clarify the kind of social life you want, and don't want. This question is very general and begs many other questions, particularly: What feelings? What kind of social life do I want?

I suggest you use The Ten Answers technique (page 28) with this question. Because this question is so general, it can take a long time to come up with the first answer. It took me several minutes to found my first answer. Until then, I could feel my mind busily searching everywhere it could.

? How can I feel like others care about what I say?
This begs the following questions:
- Do I argue with others too often?
- How well do I listen to others?
- Do others think I'm a good listener?
- Am I trying to be heard by people who will never listen to me?
- Can or will others care about my wishes as much as I would like them to?

? How can my feeling rejected or dejected help me?

? How can my anger help me communicate with others?

? How am I disrespecting others?
? How am I controlling others?
? How can I feel comfortable asking others if they feel disrespected or controlled by me?
No one usually feels like they're controlling or disrespecting others. This can be challenging and requires being honest with yourself. Together, these three questions beg the following question. What is more important, my opinion of when I'm disrespecting another person, or their opinion of when I'm disrespecting them?

? Once I decide it's necessary, how can I feel more comfortable rejecting someone?
? How can I reject someone in an empathic way?

? How can my feelings of hatred toward someone, help me love them?

? How can I feel comfortable with my jealousy?

? How can I feel more comfortable when others try to control me?
This begs the questions: When are people trying to control me? How do I know for sure?

? How can I feel comfortable with _____(particular person) who seems to hate me?

? How can I feel more comfortable accepting others' opinions?
? How can I feel more comfortable rejecting (not choosing) others' opinions?

? How can I feel more comfortable loving others?

**? How can I feel more comfortable loving _____
(particular person)?**
**? How can I feel comfortable when someone tells me
they love me?**
These beg the question: What is love, exactly?

**? How can my feelings about what others think of me,
help me?**
**? How can my feelings about what I think of others,
help me?**
My life probably would have been much different, and better,
if I had built memes with these questions when I was
fourteen years old.

? How can I better sense what someone else feels?

**? How can I feel relaxed and warm toward others in a
way they will enjoy and still be true to me?**

? How can I be an extrovert--the life of the party?

For a related discussion, see: ENGAGING BODILY
SENSATIONS ABOUT OTHER PEOPLE, page 102.

Basic Personal Exercises

**? How can my feelings help with my current desires or
needs?**
? How can my feelings help with my current goals?
Of course, those questions implicitly ask the more detailed
questions: what feelings and what desires or goals. By
repeatedly asking questions like these, your mind will
naturally start looking for those details.

Asking questions in this way also exposes the questions
you've already been asking yourself. If you're depressed,
you're probably asking yourself something like:
- Why do I have to feel this way?
- How can I make these feelings go away?
Questions like those will likely create internal conflict and
pain.

34

Noticing the questions you usually ask yourself, helps point you toward better questions. If you notice you're fighting feelings of depression, you might ask how your feelings of depression can help you with your goals and desires. For anxious fear (not for real fear like a bear walking into your living room), you could ask how you can use those feelings to resolve the situation. Or, if you decide you can't resolve it, how can you feel comfortable walking away and not resolving the situation?

Moods

? How can this mood help me do anything I want?
This implicitly asks the questions:
- What is my mood?
- What do I want?

It connects your feelings (mood) with your goals. Other implicit questions might be: Is my mood trying to tell me something? Is my confusion, anger, or my lack of skill in this situation causing this mood? Am I really powerless or am I misperceiving something?

For this question and exercise, try to find a reason that's completely new. These exercises are primarily about activating your mind and building better memes. Thinking you already know the cause of your mood just gets in the way of exploration. It's frequently a way of avoiding feelings. Let's face it, we rarely know the exact cause of our moods. We usually think emotional pain causes our moods. You might feel neglected or disrespected. You might feel powerless or ineffectual. Maybe there's a different cause. Maybe you're just physically and emotionally tired from over activity or poor health.

Try using the above question when you're in a good mood. The first time I tried that, the results were completely unexpected, interesting, and worthwhile.

For related techniques, see:
EXTREMES, page 125

35

GETTING A HANDLE ON EMOTIONS, page 81
USING QUESTIONS TO FOCUS ON BODILY SENSATIONS,
page 45
CONNECTIONS AND ASSOCIATIONS, page 47

Cravings

? How can this craving fit with all of my feelings and everything else I'm experiencing?
? How can this craving help me even if it never goes away?
These are useful when you don't want to satisfy a craving or give into it. These questions create a meme that doesn't fight any craving or set up internal conflict. These questions make no attempt to make a craving go away. They fully embrace a craving by looking for how it can help with anything else you want to do.

See: ENGAGING AND INDULGING IMPULSES, page 63, and WORKING WITH HUNGER, page 94

? How can I enjoy this _____ (craving) even more?
This is for when you decide to indulge a craving. Getting ever better at satisfying a craving is important for enjoying your life. It also helps to dispel the idea that you're being bad or weak when you indulge a craving. Stuffing yourself with food until you feel like a beached whale is fine as long as you don't do it too often.

? How else can I satisfy this craving (other than giving into it)?
The previous questions can work well with normal cravings. However, they aren't practical with the cravings from addictions like smoking cigarettes or using heroin. This question works well with cravings associated with physical addiction.

I'll use cigarettes as an example since I have experience with them. This question helped make me aware of ideas like: switching to cigarettes that only contain tobacco, exercising more, and using deep breathing exercises. I didn't think of those ideas myself. As a result of practicing this question, I was just more attentive whenever I heard someone give advice. Together, those methods finally got me to the point where cigarettes weren't part of my day. When applying this question to my overeating, I soon discovered there are many healthier ways to satisfy my cravings other than eating pasta, or bacon and cheese omelets.

Notice the question isn't about quitting anything. I searched for how to quit cigarettes for many years without success. I'm sure I set up many internal conflicts by doing that. I'd respond to the cravings with questions like:
- Why am I so weak?
- What's wrong with me?

The trick is to find things you can do that happen to reduce physical cravings. You don't have to quit doing anything. However, I don't think it's a trick at all. It's just psychology that works. Trying to quit anything doesn't work well. That usually creates internal conflict. That creates ever more anxiety.

Improving Concentration

Concentration is a mixture of focused attention and distractions. Sometimes we can focus with almost no distractions. Sometimes, especially when we're sleepy, distractions outnumber focused attention 100 to 1, or at least it seems.

Concentration blocks are usually centered on getting mad at yourself for not being able to concentrate as well as you want. For example, you have a test tomorrow and you've waited until the last minute to study for it. Your mind wants to do anything except study. You do the best you can to force yourself to concentrate but it's very frustrating and painful. Every minute or so, you think about giving up.

This technique is just finding the best mixture between focused attention and distractions for whatever you're trying to do. It's allowing your mind to wonder as much as it needs. Without this technique, you wouldn't be reading this book because it wouldn't exist. For writing, my mixture in the morning is about two parts focused attention to one part distractions. That has always been fine with me. However, in the evening, my mixture is about three parts distractions to one part focused attention. Before this technique, I would usually feel like a failure, give up, and go watch television. Now I can write for hours. At first, I thought I was more productive in the morning than later in the day. Now I see I'm just as productive but in a different way.

Whenever you notice you're getting frustrated about your ability to concentrate, ask yourself something like:
? How are all my thoughts helping me to concentrate?
How are my wandering thoughts helping my focused attention or focused thoughts? How are wandering thoughts connected to what I'm focusing on? Notice how those questions refer to "wandering thoughts" instead of distractions. The word "distraction" promotes the idea that there's a mental conflict when that's not necessarily so.

Of course, there will be times when you need to decide whether something is too overwhelming or too boring. This question can bring clarity and help you decide. Also, I've frequently found comfortable ways to focus on what I thought was overwhelming or too boring. Because I could focus more fully, I thought of better ways to accomplish something, or I realized I didn't need to do it at all.

Overwhelm and Boredom
? How can I engage this situation more comfortably?
We frequently respond to feeling overwhelmed or bored with withdrawal of attention, resistance, and pain (blocking memes). Simply trying to engage and fully focus attention, frequently cures feeling overwhelmed or bored. This question will build a meme that helps engage your attention with comfort.

Building a meme with this question is best for everyday situations like:

- feeling like you have much more to do than you can accomplish in the time you have to accomplish it
- you sense that what you need to do will be too much strain on your mind and body
- getting through boring, dull, and tedious tasks that you need to do.

Of course, there will be times when you need to decide whether something is too overwhelming or too boring. This question will help make clear when you need to decide.

Relief From Physical Tension

For at least twenty minutes, breathe as comfortably as you can. Look for any tension in your body as your chest rises and falls, and let it relax. Make your breathing as easy, efficient, and as comfortable as you can.

After about ten minutes, focus on how much or how little you need to breathe. Find where you're breathing more than you need to and where you're not breathing enough. Then try to keep it between those points.

At least for me, practicing this daily greatly improves my life. This technique directly and fully relieves tension. However, it's not always cathartic. That is, if I stop doing it, my tension comes back. However, by relaxing tension in this way, the causes of my tension become obvious. Emotions that need attention, and the best techniques to resolve them, also become more obvious.

This technique is great before bedtime for better sleep or anytime you want to relax. Do this sitting in a chair for more awareness of your feelings. If you're using it to fall asleep, laying down is best.

The Cumulative Effect of Practicing These Questions

Most of the questions focus on wondering how to be more comfortable. In time, that will become a meme. It will become automatic. You'll ask yourself questions like that subconsciously. You'll automatically connect everything in your current situation in a way that helps you feel more comfortable and engaged. Life will simply get easier and more enjoyable. A year from now you might think, "Hey! I wasn't this happy a year ago. Hmm. I wonder what changed."

CREATING OPTIONS WITH FEAR, ANGER, AND OTHER INVOLUNTARY IMPULSES

For many people (probably all), fear and anger are the primary source of discomfort, anxiety, and neurosis. Practicing the techniques in this section could resolve most of your anxiety at its core. However, this could be the most challenging section with understanding the purpose of the techniques. That is, if you've spent most of your life repressing fear or anger, you might have a difficult time practicing techniques that fully engage both. At first, you might have trouble seeing how fear and anger can be an important and useful part of your life.

This section is the pivotal point in the book. The previous techniques should give you an idea of how to unite your feelings with all other faculties of your mind. The following sections begin to build skills. They exercise your awareness and skills of all of your mind's faculties. The previous and following techniques compliment each other. The more you develop your skills, the easier it is to engage fear and anger. Engaging fear and anger gives you more tools to engage the types of issues in the previous sections.

The techniques of this section are based on the idea that fear and anger are usually involuntary responses and can't be repressed or even changed. Of course, it's possible to willfully create a fear response by thinking of something that's frightening. However, we don't usually do that. Most of our fear or anger responses happen unexpectedly whether we want them or not. Fear and anger behave like other involuntary responses from the autonomic nervous system such as: your heart rate, hunger, digestion, breathing, or sexual arousal. Repressing responses like these isn't usually possible. When it is possible, it can only be done for a short time like with holding your breath.

The primary purpose of this assumption is to help explain the techniques. I happen to think this view is accurate but there's no empirical evidence that proves it is or it isn't--and I don't think that matters. The techniques are theory neutral as any tool is. Any effect depends on how the tool is used. What matters is the effect of practicing the techniques and having a useful understanding of them.

The techniques center on creating new meme responses to fear and anger. They don't try to alter, repress, or change fear and anger. This is simply because I don't think fear or anger responses can be changed and I don't think trying to change them is helpful. Adding response options to fear and anger is more than enough to bring comfort to them and it's much easier. Working with fear and anger in this way helps you quickly recognize when you are experiencing them. They don't build to a point where they express themselves in an overwhelming, inappropriate, or embarrassing way.

For example, as a child, I was afraid to turn off the lights when going to bed. My parents assured me there were no monsters under my bed and everything would be fine. I worked at adding that assurance meme to my fear meme. After a while, I was able to turn off the lights. I created response options to my fear. Without options, I could only experience fear. Without options, I felt out of control. I wasn't only afraid of monsters; I was afraid my fear would overwhelm me. I was afraid of fear.

41

My fear wasn't destroyed. It didn't go away. On occasion, I still notice a tinge of fear when turning off the lights but my well ingrained and automatic response options immediately come to mind. That fear is now a pleasant childhood memory.

Remember the example of Jon who was angry with his wife, Marcy? First he felt anger, then wondered how he married such a bad woman, and then wondered what was wrong with him. As Jon repeated those steps, he built a meme based on his anger, physical sensations, and ideas. The stronger the meme, the faster it became. Those three steps could take a fraction of a second.

Jon set out to create a new meme by recognizing when he was angry, and then instead of fixating on the ideas that his wife is bad or he is bad, he asked:
? How can my fear and anger help me?

The more he asked that question, and the more answers he found, the more he developed a meme that was useful for interacting with his wife. He no longer repressed his anger so it didn't build to the point of yelling at his wife. Once, when he was raging with anger, he just looked at his wife and kept asking himself how his anger could be useful. Then he spontaneously and sternly said, "I hate when you interrupt me. It makes me feel like you're not interested in what I have to say."

Marcy said, "I'm interested in what you have to say, I just get enthusiastic sometimes. Why do you feel hurt about that?"

Sensing Marcy was trying to invalidate or just ignore his feelings, Jon said, "I don't want to debate whether my feelings are right or wrong. I just wish you wouldn't interrupt me."

Marcy was dumbfounded and just said, "OK."

Jon was also dumbfounded. His response, and how easily it came, surprised him. It felt like his anger guided his words as if it always knew what to say, it just needed a chance.

Jon realized ever more how his anger can be useful. When he repressed his anger, he had no access to what it was telling him so he couldn't communicate it to Marcy. When he repressed it, he also tried to repress Marcy. He just wanted her to stop doing anything that made him angry.

Being curious about his anger created a safe and easy way to access it. After a month or so, Jon and Marcy no longer fought with each other. They were more likely to laugh when one did something that annoyed the other.

The following questions create memes that look for options. They fully accept and expect the feelings and reactions of fear and anger.

? How can I feel more comfortable with my anger?
? How can I feel more comfortable with my fear?

? How else can I respond to this anger?
? How else can I respond to this fear?

? What can my anger show me?
? What can my fear show me?
? How can my fear help me feel comfortable in the world?

? How can I express my fear/anger differently?
? How is either useful?

? How can I respond differently to others' fear or anger?
? How can another's fear or anger be useful to me?

That's basically it! You can also apply these questions, and questions like these, to other involuntary responses such as: hunger, embarrassment (fear of rejection), or sexual arousal.

If you want to just connect more, or be more aware of your fear or anger, you might like these.

? How can I move an object in the room with my anger?
This is fanciful and I particularly enjoy it. It strongly reverses the idea, and response, that anger should be repressed.

? How can I be more afraid?

? If my anger, or fear, is a 7 on a 1-10 scale, how can I make it an 8?

A SUGGESTION

Don't read the rest of the book until you feel a hunger to go deeper into the techniques already discussed. Or, don't practice the following techniques until you have some experience and proficiency with the previous techniques.

With the techniques so far, it's like you've learned how to play one song on the piano. With the following techniques, it's like learning several different types of music, and how to read and write music.

After working with the above techniques, you'll likely want to go deeper and look for memes that are usually hidden. The following techniques will develop the skills you need to do that.

So far, the techniques have used mental techniques that direct attention toward bodily sensations. Many of the following techniques assume you can focus directly on bodily sensations without needing a question or other mental technique. If you still need to use a mental technique, feel free to create a question or anything that will help. Sometimes, directly focusing on bodily sensations, no matter how long you've practiced, can still be difficult.

So far, most of the techniques have included an indirect focus on bodily sensations. For many of the techniques in the rest of the book, bodily sensations are the primary focus.

You could think of these techniques as training or calisthenics, like practicing scales on a piano or football practice drills. Piano scales are not music but they greatly help with playing any song. Football drills are not the game, but they create strength and skill for playing the game.

Cautions

The following techniques can enable you to direct more attention toward your physical sensations than you ever could before. Focusing on physical sensations can bring repressed emotions into awareness that are associated with physical sensations.

If that sounds like something that would cause discomfort, or more specifically, unwanted discomfort, you might want to practice the previous techniques until you feel ready for these.

I believe that focusing on any bodily sensation directly is a powerful and fast way to relieve anxiety. Simply put, it might be too fast with some types of strong anxiety or trauma. Any self-guided technique might not be suitable for dealing with intense anxiety or trauma. If you have any doubts, consider working with a therapist. Also see, I CAN'T DO THAT. IT WOULD BE TOO PAINFUL, page 67. And see, What Catharsis Does and Doesn't Do, page 138.

USING QUESTIONS TO FOCUS ON BODILY SENSATIONS

Apply the following questions, or questions like these, to any bodily sensation you choose. You can do this anywhere, although a quiet and calm place is ideal.
? Where exactly is it located?
? How do I need this sensation?
? How does it help me?
? Is it helping me but I haven't seen how yet?
? Has it changed at all from one second ago?
? Is it continually changing?

? What about this sensation haven't I experienced or felt before?
? How can I feel it more?
? How can I let it connect to every part of me?
? How can I connect this sensation to anything else (anything in the room, the world, and so on)?
? How does this sensation connect to other sensations?
? How long have I had this sensation? How long will I have this sensation?

Questions like these will naturally direct your attention toward your sensations and put your mind in search mode. Your attention might only stay on the sensation for a fraction of a second, then immediately go to a thought, emotion, craving, or impulse. That is normal. Take note of any impulses, thoughts, or emotions, and ask about your sensations again. Then get another fraction of a second of directly focusing on a sensation. Instead of feeling distracted by thoughts or emotions, ask how they connect to your sensations. That way, your thoughts and emotions won't be distractions. If you get a thought that seems useful, write it down, then sense more bodily sensations.

Using Your Most Prominent Physical Sensation

Focus on your current most prominent sensation. It can be painful or pleasurable. It can be as simple as the sensation of your back against a chair, feeling your temples pulsate with every heartbeat, or where you most feel anxiety in your body. Ask the questions above to focus attention on the sensation. When you notice a different sensation has become prominent, focus on that.

Looking for Your Least Intense Sensation

The first time I looked for my least intense sensation, it felt odd and it was fascinating. I realized I had never before looked for my least intense sensation. Being aware of my most intense sensation is natural and easy. Looking for my least intense sensations can seem unnatural, but it's an effective way to bring all sensations into awareness. To do this, you need to take inventory of your entire body.

With this technique, I frequently end up focusing on my most intense sensation because it becomes so obvious. When I gain some comfort with that, I focus again on my least intense sensation.

Usually, when looking for my least intense sensation, I find a part of my body that has no sensation or seems numb. However, I'll likely begin to feel subtle and interesting sensations if I keep directing my attention toward that part of my body.

CONNECTIONS AND ASSOCIATIONS

Asking yourself questions automatically puts pieces of information together in new and different ways. Any new answers you get are the result of new or different connections. New patterns of neurons fire in your brain. With the exercises in this section, you should be able to gain more skill and more options with how you associate anything, including how you associate or connect with life.

Examples of Association Patterns

My process for making coffee has about twenty steps, and I do them in the same order every day. It's a strong personal meme. However, I couldn't write those steps down unless I made coffee. I need the sensory associations of standing at my stove and reaching for the coffee pot, then the coffee filters, and so on.

I have trouble remembering phone numbers unless I can see the keypad on the phone. I remember them by imagining a sequential pattern on the keypad. If someone asks me for a phone number, I need to find a phone and imagine punching the keys in order.

I remember my password for bank cash machines by using the letters on the keypad to spell my password. Even though it's the same type of keypad as a phone, I don't use a sequential pattern in that case. Once I went to a bank machine that only had numbers on the keypad, and I couldn't remember my password.

Mnemonics usually don't work for me. I have trouble remembering phrases like: **M**y **V**ery **E**ducated **M**other **J**ust **S**erved **U**s **N**ine **P**izzas. For many people that would work well to remember the planets in our solar system: **M**ercury, **V**enus, **E**arth, **M**ars, **J**upiter, **S**aturn, **U**ranus, **N**eptune, and **P**luto. I remember the planets by picturing them in order with various sizes and colors.

These are examples of association memes. If I listed a hundred or so of these examples, you could see what faculties of mind I use to associate information. You could see how often I use sensory associations or visual associations. Likewise, if you listed a hundred or so examples, you'd begin to see the patterns you use. However, there's no exercise to try to determine the patterns you currently use. There's no need. Those will become obvious while practicing new patterns.

Grouping

Grouping is simply how the elements of any experience are connected or associated in your mind. Before the bear walked into Bob's living room, Bob had a particular grouping of his experience with his living room. That included feeling relaxed, the visceral sense of sitting in his chair, the pictures on the wall, the noises outside, and so on. After his experience with the bear, Bob had a completely different grouping that consisted of a strong blocking meme and little else. After Bob's catharsis, he recovered his previous grouping and added the bear to it.

A roller coaster is not in Bob's grouping of his living room. Bob doesn't associate any part his experience riding a roller coaster with his living room. If a roller coaster appeared on his television, he would associate it with just one of the many things that can appear on his television. He wouldn't associate a real roller coaster with his living room.

As I've said previously, the mind is pliable. We can associate and group together anything with anything else. For example, think of an elephant wearing plaid pants and playing tennis with a grapefruit wearing a tuxedo. I'd bet you've never put those things together before. But, you say, that's just a silly thought. That would never become a meme that's part of anyone's life. Well, if that elephant and grapefruit were major characters in a comic strip, it would become a large part of the cartoonist's life.

? How can my feelings connect with all that is happening in a way that creates something new and useful?
To practice this question, you would need to fill in the specifics of your life and other association elements like time and space. Does "all that is happening" refer to now, this week, or another time frame? Does it refer to all that is happening in your room, your city, or country? I've used this question extensively for writing this book. I love to write but I hate sitting in one place for long. After an hour or two of writing, I'll get strong impulses to watch TV, go outside, or a million other things. I would rather do anything than sit still and ponder what would make a better sentence. This question comfortably puts me back into the moment and the task at hand.

? How can I feel more comfortable in this room?
This question inherently creates more associations and connections to any object or person in the room.

Time
? How could I feel comfortable with this situation if it lasted the rest of my life?
? What will this situation feel like in a month, year, or five years from now?
Any change of the time frame can add needed perspective and useful associations.

Space

? How much space is around my feeling ____?
? How can I give this feeling more space?
? How can I give this feeling less space?
Whether you're aware of it or not, many feelings have a
sense of space. For example, you have an exam tomorrow.
You haven't studied for it, and failing it will probably mean
you'll need to take the class over to graduate. Which
scenario best describes that feeling?

- You're in a small box. The air is stale and difficult to
  breathe.
- You're in the middle of a breezy field with tall grass
  and you can see the horizon no matter which way you
  turn.

In general, we usually associate tension with a small
confined space, and we associate relaxation with open space.
When you're depressed, and it feels like the walls are
closing in on you, you want to close the curtains and hide
under a blanket. When you're happy, you want to go to the
park.

At first, most people find working with these questions
confusing and even unsettling, especially the last two
questions. It might feel like you shouldn't tamper with a
basic way of perceiving the world. Building memes with
these questions will give you more comfort and awareness
with a perceptual element that affects you daily. You'll begin
to notice what your mind wants to do, needs to do, and you
can help it along.

Size and Intensity

? How big and intense are my feelings?
? What is my biggest or most intense feeling?
? What is my smallest or least intense feeling?
A minor annoyance might be the size of a ping-pong ball
that you can ignore indefinitely if you want. Rage would be

about the size of a truck that you might be able to ignore but only with great difficulty.

? What is the color, sound, or texture of my feelings?
Not everyone has a visual association with feelings. This might or might not be useful for you.

Association and Bodily Sensations

Take anything you experience through your senses, internally or externally, and connect it to any bodily sensation. Find how a bodily sensation somehow connects or associates with something else.

- Externally: sounds in the room, the chair across the room, people in the room, your sense of something five miles away and so on.
- Internally: any thought, emotion, another bodily sensation, memory, anything imagined, and so on.

This is an exercise to increase awareness of your connections or groupings and to keep your attention focused on bodily sensations. The object and sensations you pick to connect can be silly. As an example, I'll just look around the room and pick something.

? How are the feelings in my left lower leg connected to my baseball hat hanging on the wall?
At first, I couldn't think of any connections but I kept searching. Ah, the memory of hitting a baseball hat against my leg to get the dust off. I think I've seen baseball players do that many times. It looks like the hat is about twelve feet from my leg at a forty-five degree angle. I got the hat at a state park after hiking up and down rocks and through streams. Hiking and feelings in my legs have many connections.

With that example, I could easily hold my attention on the sensations in my leg. There were few existing connections between my leg and the baseball hat and any emotional associations were mild.

Now I'll use an object with more connections and some associated emotion. What's in the room that fits? Ah, my winter coat. I have many visceral sensations and connections with my coat. It works well most of the time, but it isn't always as warm as I want. I like the sensations of warmth on most days. However, it has never been tight enough and I get cold on windy days.

Now I'll think of an example with many connections and strong emotional associations. Let me see. It could be the sensations in my stomach and how they associate with my spouse (who is in the next room). That immediately feels like it could be emotionally intense and have many connections and associations.

When connections with an object or person have an emotional charge, other associated sensations usually come to mind. That is, I originally picked the sensations in my stomach. As soon as I started searching for connections, I realized I had more associations with my spouse and feelings in my chest. However, after looking for connections with my chest awhile, the sensations in my jaw became prominent. Then the sensations in my stomach became prominent again.

Elements of Association

The following elements can greatly enhance, develop, or just help you enjoy your bodily sensations. More awareness and comfort with your sensations will also develop and add perspective to any associated thoughts and emotions.

- Space. What is the distance between a bodily sensation and any object in the room? What is the distance between a bodily sensation and your grocery store, where you work, a park, and so on?
- Time. How long will the sensation last? Is it already different from three seconds ago? Can it last forever? How long have you experienced it with the object you picked?

- Pain or pleasure. How painful or pleasurable is the sensation. Is there any association with an object in the room?
- Size. How big is the sensation? How much of your body does it affect? Can you make it bigger or smaller? Does an object in the room affect the size of the sensation?
- Intensity. Does the object you chose affect the intensity of the sensation? Can you increase or lessen the intensity of the sensation?
- Some people don't take to being this creative or far out, but I'm including this for those who find it useful. Does the vibration of your sensations in any way connect to the vibration of the carpet, refrigerator, lamp, other people, etc.? Sound is always vibration. How are the different sounds connecting and mingling with each other and with the vibration of your sensations?

Playing with the Elements of Association to Focus on Bodily Sensations

As an example, let's say you're shy. In your imagination, you probably see most people as bigger than you. If they're not bigger, you might see them as faster, more able to move about the room, more relaxed or more energetic. Everyone in the room connects to each other and you're outside that connection. Everyone's movements flow comfortably and yours are tense, awkward, and self-conscious. You think that you've always been shy, and you always will be shy.

Now let's play with those elements. Remember a time when you were in a room full of people. Are they shoulder to shoulder or is the room half empty? Which people dominate or stand out in the room? Which people seem the biggest regardless of their physical size? Which people seem to draw more attention and take up more space? Can you use more space in a way that is interesting to others? Who is intense, and who is barely noticeable? How intense are you compared with people near you?

53

? How can I comfortably connect to others and their thoughts and emotions?

By looking for new associations in that way, could you still be shy? Asking those questions would activate your mind's curiosity or search mode. You would look at people and observe them in much more detail than when you feel shy and afraid. The questions would start to remove blocks that limit your sensory perception. It would be much easier to think of something to say to anyone and you would be more approachable.

I constructed that scenario, and questions, from looking at the list of elements above. You can do that with any experience you can imagine. With a little practice, you can create any perspective you want and use your new perspective in helpful ways.

Belly Catharsis - Eating Everything

A baby will put anything it can grab into its mouth. It's instinctive. We constantly sense the world with our gastrointestinal system. Your stomach has an opinion about everything you do. An unpleasant situation can make you nauseous. When someone talks about something they strongly dislike, they might say, "I can't stomach that." Stress and anxiety can cause overeating or loss of appetite.

This technique is to use your imagination to eat everything in your general vicinity. Eat the couch, the television, the carpet, the microwave, the refrigerator, the toaster, and so on. The purpose of this exercise is to activate and focus on sensations in your digestive system. If it will make it easier, you can skip the part about tasting, chewing, and swallowing your toaster, or any object you can't really eat. Just imagine taking the toaster into your stomach and digesting it.

? How can I digest the _____ (sofa, table, carpet, etc.)?

Over time, you've probably become unaware of how your stomach reacts when you accept or resist an experience. Maybe you're uncomfortable with the different types of hungers you experience. Maybe you have a tendency to confuse hunger for life with hunger for food. Maybe you have a habit of avoiding hunger because you don't want to overeat, but somehow, you overeat anyway and feel anxious about it. Maybe you feel hungry because you focus much attention on the taste of food, but little attention on the sensations of food in your stomach. In that case, your brain doesn't fully know that you've satisfied your hunger so you keep eating until you're bloated.

? How can my hunger help me (whether I feed it or not)?
Using this question is just a way to bring all of your hungers back into your awareness in an accepting way. Unlike when you were a baby, no one will yell at you to get that out of your mouth. It will reconnect your awareness of your stomach to all of your experience. Awareness directed toward your stomach causes any tension in your stomach to relax. A comfortable gastrointestinal system won't keep sending hunger signals to your brain if you're not hungry, and it won't suppress your appetite.

This, more than anything I've tried, has enabled me to eat as much food as I really want, and no more. I've become more aware of, and connected to, my gastrointestinal system. I usually eat only to fulfill my body's hunger. When I'm hungry for life, I eat life. Practicing this question made those feel natural and easy.

Eating People Using Your Imagination (not particularly in the erotic sense)

As with the exercise listed above, this is for activating and focusing on the sensations in your stomach that can occur when you stomach someone, so to speak.

Practicing this technique had effects that I didn't expect at all. Most of my life, I haven't been very approachable. I've always been shy and slightly uncomfortable with anyone I don't know well. Without expecting it, my discomfort went away. Suddenly, clerks in stores were smiling at me. The grumpy (or so I thought) people at the post office joked around with me. It was as if they felt acceptance from me on a gut level. Suddenly, I could stomach people that I couldn't before. I could disagree with them without getting testy and annoyed with them. So, I could spend much more time disagreeing with them. Because of that, I had the opportunity to see that I don't disagree with them as much as I thought.

I know how far fetched that might sound but consider how focused animals are with hunger and the gastrointestinal system. Animals spend most of their time searching for food. In some ways, so do humans, even when a wide variety of food is always available.

For contrast, you might try the opposite of this exercise. Don't digest your surroundings in anyway. Nothing gets past your lips. Keep everything out of your stomach. When I first tried that, I noticed how my stomach moves with every inhale. Since my inhale brings something into me, literally and figuratively, a conflict developed between my breathing and my stomach. I tried this only a handful of times and felt far too much anxiety to do it longer than a few minutes. I wondered if it would be a useful technique for an actor who wanted to play an angry character because it created much anger in me.

Also, you can try to get a sense of people eating you. When you're with someone who is shy and uncomfortable, try to sense what their experience is in a gastrointestinal sense? For the other extreme, how is someone stomaching you, when that person talks constantly and barely listens to anything you say?

Planning to Feel Anxiety All Day

The paradox is you want your anxiety to go away, but the best way to make it go away is to fully embrace it--and stop trying to make it go away. Planning to feel your anxiety all day takes skill and faith, especially if the anxiety is strong. It takes skill to convince your mind that you sincerely want to feel something all day. It takes faith that doing that will have the outcome you want. That is, your anxiety turns into comfort.

Frequently for me, if other techniques don't cause a catharsis, this technique quickly does. My mind sees planning to indulge a feeling as the complete opposite of resisting the feeling. If I'm planning it, resistance isn't possible.

It almost never takes a full day to have a relaxing catharsis with this method. It usually takes just minutes once you've sincerely convinced yourself that you're completely willing to feel it all day, or for as long as it takes. But you can't lie to yourself. You can't say you will do it all day, but really want catharsis to happen quickly. Your mind knows when you are insincere. Your primitive mind knows when you're resisting it to any degree. I find this phenomenon interesting and amusing, even after having experienced it many times. I frequently catch myself being insincere. Once I correct this, catharsis soon follows.

How can you turn insincerity into sincerity? First, assume that you already know how. You've probably done it many times before and if you try, you'll naturally access the method that works for you. In addition, the more sensory detail you can add to the scenes you imagine, the more real it will seem. By sensory detail, I mean details like colors or patterns, sounds, smells, or something felt on your skin or body.

It's best to do this technique with eyes closed and sitting down. Start by imagining all that you'll be doing and all the places you will go throughout the day. Think of the times when you'll be doing something that doesn't need your full attention, and you can focus on your sensations. Use questions to steer your attention toward your sensations. Even though this is all in your imagination, don't plan to focus on sensations while doing anything dangerous like driving a car.

Here's an example that includes planning to feel anxiety all day. There's much tension between you and your boss. You love your job, but you're ready to quit because of the daily discomfort you feel with your boss. You've tried everything you can think of to get along with your boss, but it seems as if your personalities just don't mix.

You go to work feeling the anxiety you usually feel, but this time you plan to feel it all day. You don't try to avoid meetings with your boss as you usually do; instead, you wonder how you can increase the intensity of your anxiety.

You notice that you feel a combination of fear and anger. You feel tightness in your chest, and you work to exaggerate that sense of tightness. You notice how you're reluctant to inhale, and you follow that reluctance until you feel like you want to curl up in a ball on the floor. You feel like you want to cry.

Your boss stops by to talk to you about something. You immediately notice how different you feel. Usually when you see your boss, you feel anxiety and discomfort and wish you didn't. Normally, you can't wait until your boss goes away, but this time it's different. You still feel the anxiety and discomfort, but now you're trying to feel it. You're interested in it. For the first time, you are fully engaging the bodily sensations of the anxiety. It feels weird to fully engage your anxiety while interacting with your boss, but it's also fascinating.

When you see your boss throughout the day, you notice your discomfort changing. You can't explain it, but something is happening. Memories from childhood pop into your head that seem associated to your anxiety. You keep trying to feel the anxiety you normally feel about your boss, but after a while it becomes an effort. You start to feel bored with the whole thing.

A week passes. You've just had a meeting with your boss. It occurs to you that you weren't anxious at all during this meeting. Your boss was friendly. He even told a couple of jokes and seemed relaxed. You're still not sure if you like your boss, but it's becoming easy to interact with him or her. It dawns on you that much of the problem you had with your boss was because you were tense. Maybe your boss reacted to your tension and anxiety. Maybe that was the problem all along. You're not sure, but it no longer matters to you. You're just happy to be comfortable.

Indulging Depression - Intentional Disassociation

This exercise is purposely indulging depression and disassociating from everything. It can be very restful. Don't try this if:

- You don't intuitively understand that feeling down, on purpose, is a viable way to handle feeling down.
- You feel that indulging blue or depressed feelings could make you feel worse.
- You have chronic depression. This technique, with the association techniques above, could help with chronic depression but you should probably discuss it with a professional (see, Cautions, page 45).

The next time you feel depressed, crawl into bed and tell the world to go away. Be nothing. Be blank. Let the weight of the world push you into the mattress. Don't try to get up or push against it. Let everything overwhelm you. Let your world fall apart. Give up. Lose the game. Lose the fight.

? How can my feelings of depression help me?

? How do my depressed thoughts connect to my sensations?
However, you might not have many thoughts. Feeling down or depressed is one of the few times when the thinking mind turns off, and your bodily sensations fill awareness.

If you've never done this before, it can feel liberating. Resistance to feeling depressed can be most of the pain of feeling depressed. When resistance is suddenly gone, you'll feel great relief. Intentionally feeling depressed is so different from feeling depressed and resisting it. You no longer need to spend energy trying to fix it. You no longer need to wonder what is wrong with you. Now, your thinking mind is open to a better understanding of anything that contributes to your feelings.

Why do we feel depressed? I certainly don't know but I find the following viewpoint helpful. Feeling down or depressed, is a form of exhaustion from strong emotion or long term subtle unwanted emotion. You need rest. Giving into the blues is a direct way to get that rest. It lets your parasympathetic nervous system do its job (see, THE AUTONOMIC NERVOUS SYSTEM, page 161). Resisting feeling down just prolongs the exhaustion.

You also might want to approach the feelings as a genetic or old memory (see, GENETIC MEMORY, page 74).

Jack Wants to Ask Anabel for a Date

This next example has a particular subject that uses the element of association. However, you can apply the elements of association to any experience.

When referred to, a specific element will be in parentheses. A parenthetical ellipsis (...), indicates when Jack focuses on his bodily sensations.

(...) I won't know what to say. I'll stammer and say something stupid. I'll feel about as much stress as jogging, but much less than playing basketball with Dan who usually beats me (comparison, pain or pleasure--jogging or basketball can be either). Hmm. I'll tell her I'll probably say something stupid. That would help.

Where do I feel the stress (space)? (...) Kind of all over but my chest mostly. My heart and breathing are speeding up. Some adrenaline must be kicking in. Can I make the sensations more intense (intensity)? (...) I'm not sure. The sensations seem more intense but being more aware of them might cause that. Can I make the sensation bigger (size)? It doesn't seem so. The sensations are what they are, but asking that directed my attention toward them. How do my sensations connect to the kitchen table (connection)? They sort of do but I can't explain how. As if the space between me and the table connects both somehow.

(...) How long can I feel this (time)? Can I feel it until I ask her for a date? Yeah, I suppose I can. It's not that bad.

(...) Can I connect my sensations to the scene in general and to Anabel no matter how she reacts (connection)? What if she gets angry? What if she gets uncomfortable? What if she smiles and says, yes, of course I'd like a date with you?

Wow! That did it, a catharsis. With all my fear, discomfort, and resistance, I never thought about it from Anabel's point of view. All I have to do is let her react anyway she wants. If she feels uncomfortable, I can help her. I can tell her it's fine if she doesn't want to go out with me. I'll understand. OK, so that's not entirely true but what else can I say? I know, I'll tell her I'll be devastated, but I won't be devastated for long. That is true and it would probably make her laugh. Come to think of it, I'm not really prepared if she says yes. I better think about that. I better focus on my sensations about that.

Working with the elements of association helps with creating catharsis, because the elements direct awareness toward bodily sensations. It's easy to focus on the ideas Jack had and become sidetracked, but the real action is in the ellipsis when Jack focused on his sensations. Without that focus, catharsis wouldn't have occurred. The useful ideas and revelations Jack had probably wouldn't have occurred either.

Free Association

? How does this sensation connect to _____?
Freely connect anything to anything else, without concern for logic or if the connections make sense. For example,

61

what is the distance between a bodily sensation and a picture on the wall? Associate and connect your sensation with any memory of the picture. Where did you first get it? Where will the picture be a year from now--five years or one hundred years? Does associating the picture with your sensation, change the sensation in any way? Do that with any object in the room that you see, hear, or feel.

If a memory pops into your head, ask yourself how that might connect to a bodily sensation, then ask yourself how your memory and your sensation might connect to an object in the room.

If you realize you're fantasizing about something, ask yourself how that fantasy might connect to a bodily sensation. Then ask yourself how the fantasy and your sensations might connect to an object in the room.

If you have an emotion, ask yourself where you feel that emotion in your body. Then ask yourself how the emotion and the sensation in your body connect to an object in the room. Notice, I didn't mention trying to analyze or define the emotion.

As with most of these exercises, there is no such thing as a distraction or doing it incorrectly. As soon as you realize you're off somewhere in fantasy land, just ask yourself how that fantasy connects to a sensation and something in the room. If you use a fantasy, thought, or emotion as part of your focus, than inherently it's not a distraction.

Most people agree that living in the present is desirable. But it's so easy to become wrapped up in our thoughts and lose sight of what being in the moment means. For me, this exercise usually brings to mind the following:
- I can think about other places but I can only do that here.
- I can remember the past and ponder the future, but I can only do that now.

I think this exercise is especially good for experience that is outside your normal routine, or for adjusting to a new situation. Let's say you've moved to a new house, apartment, or college dormitory. It was clear to you that you needed to move, but emotionally you didn't want to move. You were happy where you were.

You're sitting in your new home. You have mostly settled in. Most of the boxes are gone and the place is getting comfortable, but you keep thinking about your previous home. You'd rather be there. However, you've read this book so you try this exercise.

Most everywhere you look, you see something that was in your previous home. Let's say you're looking at an old toothpick holder that your grandmother gave you. You focus fully on the memory of the toothpick holder and where it was in your previous home. You connect that memory with the first bodily sensation you notice, and then you connect both to your view of the toothpick holder in your new home. It feels weird at first, but after several minutes, you begin to relax. At some point, you get the sense that your grandmother doesn't care where the toothpick holder is, as long as it reminds you of her. Even though your grandmother isn't alive, your thought is somehow comforting. After some time, you feel better. You start thinking, and more importantly feeling, that your previous home was great but this new place has potential.

ENGAGING AND INDULGING IMPULSES

The following techniques for indulging an impulse are based on the idea that your subconscious, your autonomic nervous system, or whatever generates cravings and fears, doesn't know the difference between reality and your imagination (see, HOW THE REPTILIAN, MAMMALIAN, AND THINKING MINDS INTERACT AND AFFECT EACH OTHER, page 168). To put it another way, your primitive brain has a mind of its own and doesn't know that it, and your thinking mind, are part of the same self. If it did, you wouldn't feel fear simply by thinking about something fearful. Your primitive mind would know that you're only thinking about something fearful and there's nothing to fear. Indulging impulses unites your thinking mind and your primitive mind.

? How can this impulse help me?
For example, imagine walking by a bakery and noticing your favorite cake in the window. Now you have a strong craving for some of that cake, but you think you should resist that impulse. Instead of feeling anxious that you once again have a craving that you must control, you stand at the window. You imagine sticking your fingers into the moist cake and putting some in your mouth. You do that for as long as you want, and then walk away smiling. You have fully acknowledged your craving instead of resisting it. You don't feel weak for having it in the first place. You don't have internal conflict from starting a fight with yourself.

Of course, eating cake and imagining eating cake are very different experiences. Unless you have a good imagination, eating cake is going to stimulate your senses far more than eating cake in your imagination. However, imagining eating cake without really eating it satisfies the craving enough. It doesn't go into battle mode. You don't keep fighting yourself until you give in and actually eat cake. We frequently give into a craving just to relieve the painful internal conflict.

Indulging an impulse works best in real time situations. It works best with cravings or impulses that distract your concentration and your effectiveness in general. It's a quick way to accept, rather than resist an impulse and gain some comfort with it. If you then want to explore the impulse for achieving a catharsis, the association and questioning techniques are probably best.

The more you practice this, the more impulses stop fighting you. They become suggestions or just ideas that you can decide to follow or not, instead of something that gnaws at you constantly. By engaging impulses, you don't need to control them. Your subconscious sees that you accept the impulses it wants to give you and stops nagging you for attention.

The Basic Steps for Indulging an Impulse

- awareness of an impulse (craving, fear, anger)
- engage and indulge the impulse with a detailed focus on bodily sensations
- ask how the impulse can help you do anything you're trying to do

For example, let's use constant cravings for fatty food. First, engage and indulge the craving. Think about fatty foods for as long as you can. Imagine eating them being sure to imagine the physical sensation of eating those foods. The more sensory detail you can add the better. Imagine cheesy pizza in your mouth. Where's the nearest pizza place and what hours are they open? Imagine chocolate melting on your tongue. Where's the nearest candy store? What was your last meal? Can you still feel it in your stomach?

? How can my cravings help with what I'm doing now?
Notice your current sensations and associate those with anything near you. That brings you back into your activity the craving interrupted. Then associate fatty foods with anything in your current situation. Imagine a steamy delicious pizza right in front of you. Imagine how nibbling on the pizza would help you with your current activities or goals. If you aren't doing something in particular that the craving interrupted, you can indulge the craving until you become bored with it, or imagine doing something else that you might like to do.

Now you have fully accepted your bodily sensations associated with the craving. You've also fully accepted the sensations of your current activity. You can comfortably choose either one. The perceived conflict between your impulse and your current activity is gone. Any resistance the conflict might have created toward the impulse, or toward your current activity, is also gone.

Impulsive Fear and Anger

? How can my fear or anger help with anything I want to do?

Fear and anger are usually spontaneous and involuntary. You can indulge them in the same way as the craving example above. Also, applying the genetic memory theory can be useful for gaining comfort and awareness with fear and anger (see GENETIC MEMORY, page 74).

I CAN'T DO THAT - IT WOULD BE TOO PAINFUL. TECHNIQUES THAT HELP WITH RESISTANCE AND BLOCKS

In general, your mind can and will defend itself no matter what you do. Trust the questions and focuses your mind picks. Your mind won't pick something you can't handle. If you're worried about doing the techniques, your mind is already defending itself. Focusing on something that you've always found pleasant can work just as well as focusing on something unpleasant. It doesn't need to be unpleasant (see, CATHARSIS AND PLEASURE, page 26). You can certainly achieve catharsis--more catharsis--with something you already accept and like.

Like with physical exercise, it's just a matter of not going too far. Experiencing too much pain usually develops an aversion to doing something. Like with physical exercise, when you can do it at a comfortable level, it feels good and you'll want to do it often. It might feel uncomfortable to some degree while you're doing it, but more and more, you see how good it makes you feel the rest of the time. The more you turn anxiety into comfort, the more you will want to do it.

THIS BOOK IS CRAP - THE AUTHOR IS AN IDIOT

If you need to think that and it works, why not? I'm sure you'll think that anyway if you need to.

BEING A FLY ON THE WALL

If practicing a cathartic technique is throwing you into a painful emotional tizzy, but you feel you want to continue, this can work quite well. Just view the scene from a different place. In your imagination, watch yourself and anyone else in the scene from a safe distance or a safe place. Go to the corner of the room near the ceiling where no one can see you and watch yourself and everyone else. Try to see what caused or is causing you to feel anxious, threatened, or tense. This change of perspective can be very useful whether you're in an emotional tizzy or not.

Here's a personal example with using the fly-on-the-wall technique. In junior high school, other kids teased me on occasion. I usually became paralyzed and had no idea how to respond. That usually caused more teasing. It was very painful. After going back to the scene as a fly on the wall, I could take a comfortable look around. I saw how the main perpetrator was a short pudgy kid. He attacked everyone he could because he would get laughs and attention primarily from a particular teacher. I guess that was power, back then. I wonder how that kid turned out.

By remembering that experience, and asking questions about the associated bodily sensations, I felt a strong catharsis. It gave me comfort with those memories and when anyone teases me in any way. Feeling anxious about that memory seems silly now, but apparently it was something I still had emotions about and still resisted.

RESISTANCE AND REPRESSION ON PURPOSE

From everything discussed so far, you might get the impression that diverting attention from thoughts and emotions (repression) is bad. It's not. Diversion and repression are important and necessary skills. We use them every day at our job, in social situations, or when we feel anxiety for any reason. We put off fully feeling anxiety until we have a chance to mull it over. Then we vent the pressures we feel, and feel better because of it. Diversion and repression only become a problem when they are habitual, not optional, and don't help you in any way.

If the struggle between focusing on a sensation and its resistance seems too strong, resist the sensation on purpose. Play around with ignoring sensations and even repress them. That will likely bring some relief. Then, focus on the sensation again. You can repeat this for as long as needed.

However, as you'll probably see, you can't truly resist an experience on purpose. Spontaneous resistance and conscious resistance are very different. True resistance is involuntary, impulsive, and barely conscious. Conscious and willful resistance requires that you decide how to resist an experience. Do you divert your attention and think of something else? Do you hold your body still to prevent any reactions and wait for the impulse to go away? Do you tense your body and grit your teeth? Resisting a sensation on purpose still directs some awareness toward the sensation you're trying to resist. So, you're still focusing on the sensation to some degree.

However, resisting the sensation on purpose still brings relief from any sense of struggle. It's as if you've tricked your subconscious into thinking you're back with the familiar habit of avoiding the experience.

At very least, this technique is a great way to keep from resisting resistance. If you take an intentional look at your own resistance and diversion, you can more quickly recognize when you're resisting something, even when it's true spontaneous involuntary resistance.

REMEMBER WHERE YOU ARE

Let's say you're at home. Unless your house suddenly falls down, you're perfectly safe. No matter what emotions or sensations you bring to awareness, you're in a safe place.

No matter what you imagine, no matter what you feel, the reality is you are at home and safe. There is no danger in imagining or feeling anything you want.

I've found remembering this throughout the day to be very beneficial. I've realized how safe I am most of the time. There are no problems at all. The biggest and most persistent danger we have is automobile traffic. Several times a day, we're inches away from being injured, maimed, or killed from a traffic accident.

SEPARATION ANXIETY

Trying to separate or suppress parts of your mind can make focusing on anything especially difficult and cause much anxiety. It usually starts an energy-draining struggle within you. For example, you might think that anything that pops into your awareness other than your primary focus is a distraction, and you need to expel it from your mind before you can fully focus.

Distractions can be internal, such as rambling thoughts or emotions; they can also be external, such as birds chirping outside or some other noise. Unwanted thoughts can be most distracting. They can cause frustration and a futile effort to control your thoughts.

You don't need to have distractions. Instead, unite all of your experience toward the same goal.
? How can this "distraction" connect to everything?
Look for how your rambling thoughts or emotions can help with anything you're trying to do. Look for how your thoughts connect to your sensations. If you don't see any connections, just let your thoughts and emotions run in the background and check back with them occasionally. Maybe they're helping and you just haven't seen how yet.

Here's another technique: Imagine your thoughts, outside noises, or any other distraction, all in the same room as your primary focus. For example, imagine that your focus on a sensation is the chair you're sitting on, and that your thoughts are over by the bookcase, rambling on as usual. Your emotions are breezing around the room with the circulating air. This way, everything in the room becomes part of your focus, yet the sensation you're working with remains as your primary focus. With this psychological trick, you don't need to feel distracted or fight with your thoughts or emotions. And you don't have to deal with their fighting back.

Even so, sometimes your thinking mind just won't shut up, so focusing is difficult. When this happens, you can get the thinking mind to calm down by indulging it or by overwhelming it. One way to do this is with continuous writing, as described on page 124. Another way is to walk fast, or do any other aerobic exercise for about twenty minutes.

A Concentration Exercise

The following technique is like taking your mind to the gym and working out. It strengthens your mind just as working out with weights strengthens your muscles. It increases your ability to concentrate in a relaxed manor and without internal conflict.

Sit in a comfortable position and concentrate on something for at least twenty minutes. Constantly look for details you haven't seen before. Whenever you become aware of a thought or anything that isn't the subject of your focus, a-- "distraction"--find how it fits with your focus or how it's trying to help with your focus. In other words, there's no such thing as a distraction.

I usually concentrate on something sensory like music (with eyes closed), a picture, a candle, or something physical like air flowing against my skin (a fan on low helps with this). This is also a powerful way to work with a Core Catharsis question, or to contemplate anything.

MORE TECHNIQUES

PICK ANY MEMORY

Pick a memory, any memory. Go there in your imagination. Experience it again. Focus on all aspects of it.

? How can I comfortably experience this memory?
Working with memories is relatively easy. Focusing on the sensations of a memory frequently brings to mind more details about the memory without altering it. After you have a catharsis, the memory will become just a matter of record. You can examine more of its details. You can ponder what it means to you to any degree you want. The memory will no longer be a source of anxiety; it will come and go freely as you're reminded of it.

The memory you pick can be pleasurable or painful. Notice any bodily sensations that seem associated with your memory and use questions that focus attention to your sensations. Use the memory enough to stimulate bodily sensations that seem associated with the memory, but primarily focus on the sensations, not the memory. Add another detail about the memory and notice how your sensations change. Also notice how your thoughts and emotions change.

Caution. While focusing on bodily sensations, an associated memory can come to mind that seems like a recovered memory. You might feel that you've released a memory stored in the tension of a sensation that you've never remembered before. Since there's usually no way to know, you can't be sure how accurate any memory is that seems released. The mind can easily associate experience with anything that makes sense, whether it's true or not. It might make up memories. Think how creative your mind is while dreaming.

I think it's best to use associated memories, emotions, or thoughts, as if they were from a dream. If they help you, great, but getting fixated on how real or true they might be, can be perilous. Also, thinking about the content of a memory centers on ideas Instead of sensations. That stops the cathartic and meme building process.

GENETIC MEMORY

Genetic memory is the idea that we are born with the basic memories of all human experience. This theory, or postulate, hasn't been proven, but that's not important. The theory is important as much as it's useful. It's useful in that it can plausibly explain strong emotions that seem like overreactions. It can explain strong emotions that don't seem connected to anything real and seem like they will last forever.

To use this theory, think of a scene that has probably happened to humans repeatedly throughout human history, where your emotions would fit. Keep in mind that civilization is a recent development in human history. Most human experience is living in a tribe as a hunter-gatherer.

For example, for no apparent reason, you have a strong fear that you will lose your job. Maybe you made a minor mistake, and now you're worrying that you'll lose your job, even though no one has ever lost their job for such a mistake. But for whatever reason, your fear is strong. Losing your job means losing your association with a group. Throughout most of human history, losing your connection with a group could easily mean you would die. If your tribe or family shunned you, you probably couldn't survive. Even if you could find enough food to feed yourself, you would still be much more vulnerable to attack from carnivorous animals.

Teenagers frequently have strong emotions if shunned by their group. In a tribal context, the adults would protect teenagers less and start demanding they take on adult responsibilities that contribute to the tribe's survival. The tribe might shun the teenager if they don't feel the teenager

74

is fulfilling their new duties. Being shunned by the tribe could be devastating for a teenager.

Another example of genetic memory is monsters. Throughout human history, animals have attacked humans, and humans have attacked each other. When attacked, we frequently exaggerate the size of the attacker. If a bear that's four feet tall attacks you, you'll experience the fight-or-flight response or go into shock. During the attack, if you see the bear it will be inches from your eyes. It would be easy to think the bear was ten feet tall. Even if you clearly saw the bear was four feet tall before it attacked, the fight, flight, or shock response would be so strong you would likely only remember that. During the attack, you'd likely only have glimpses of the bear that creates a distorted image that no longer resembles a bear. You'd come away thinking a monster attacked you.

Children have been vulnerable through most of human history. A large animal could carry them off in the night. It's no wonder they fear monsters at bedtime.

Another example is the winter blues. Sure, winter isn't as pleasant as spring, summer, or fall. Is that why you feel so down or are you tapping into human memory? Maybe you're remembering all those times we have barely survived winter. Food is scarce and difficult to get. You have to compete with carnivorous animals that would eat you given an opportunity. You've been sick for two weeks. The howling wind torments you with the cold it brings. The skies are dark and ominous. You're starving already and then a blizzard keeps you bundled up in a cave for three days.

How often have you felt rage when you thought someone wronged you? When you thought about it, their trespass was minor and they didn't mean to wrong you at all. For example, someone in front of you walks too slowly. Every time you go to pass them, they unknowingly veer in front of you. How about those idiots on their cell phones who talk too loud and have incredibly stupid conversations, or all those clowns who don't know how to drive a car, or those

75

rude people who put the toilet roll on the wrong way, or rumor has it that John said you look ugly sometimes, and so on. Does your reaction, or overreaction, come from genetic memory?

Genetic Memory and Behavior

The genetic memory theory can also explain some types of behavior. Throughout human history, how did men and women spend most of their time (and I don't mean to start a battle of the sexes)?

Men would form a group and go on hunts. They needed strong depth perception and skill for throwing rocks or spears. They needed to work together in complex ways. They needed to be aware of their surroundings almost constantly. They needed a strong sense of direction so they wouldn't get lost. Asking for directions would be a sign of incompetence. Their nonverbal communication skills would be strong. They needed to be quiet to be successful hunters and to survive. If one man talked too much, the others would likely beat or even kill him because talking would threaten their survival.

Women would spend most of their time gathering or harvesting food, and taking care of children. They would talk to their children to teach them. They would talk to scare off dangerous animals or just to pass the time. Women would develop strong verbal and interpersonal skills. They would know a great deal about each other's thoughts and feelings.

All of that seems accurate, but again, I don't know (or particularly care) how true or accurate these ideas are. I care that they're useful in understanding and interacting with the opposite sex.

So What Does the Genetic Memory Theory Have to Do With Catharsis?

Throughout much of this book, I state that focusing on bodily sensations is a great way to bring comfort to those

76

sensations. The thoughts and emotions that occur from focusing on sensations can be more accurate. Bodily sensations can reconcile, counsel, or ground thoughts and emotions.

With strong emotions, I'm making something of an exception, simply because strong emotions can make it difficult to focus on anything. Using the genetic memory theory to first get a mental handle on a strong emotion, greatly helps with focusing on the bodily sensations of the emotion.

Possibly, using the genetic memory theory is just a way to explain the unexplainable. Even if it is, it still helps to clear confusion and get a useful mental handle on emotions. Then, focusing on bodily sensations becomes easier.

Another useful quality of the genetic memory theory is it can clarify what is happening in your life. Usually, an emotion from genetic memory has some relation to something real in your life. There is something happening in your life that should concern you. You might never be exactly sure where genetic memory ends, and the reality of your situation begins, but that's probably not necessary. Pondering where the line is gets you close enough to be helpful.

Additionally, strong and confusing emotions usually occur when you're tired or excessively stressed. If you frequently have strong and confusing emotions, you might want to rest and practice any relaxation techniques that you prefer.

Extreme Genetic Memory Focuses

Examples of extreme genetic memory focuses are: decaying bodies, heads piled up on a battlefield, slavery, rape, and pillage.

I've found that focusing in detail on those extreme experiences is useful, but I can certainly understand why someone would be reluctant to apply cathartic techniques to these imagined experiences. Use your intuition to decide for yourself.

If you've actually experienced any of these, you might want to consult with a therapist before applying any cathartic techniques to them. For more on using extremes, see page 125

Jason, Kevin, and a Timber Rattlesnake

Here's a story that shows how resistance affects experience. Unlike most examples in this book, this is graphic and possibly disturbing, especially if you're like many people (me) who have a primal fear of snakes. I probably refer to snakes too often in this book, but this example covers several aspects of resistance: genetic memory, primal ingrained resistance, how resistance feeds itself, new resistance from trauma, and more. It's also symbolic in that much of our resistance is toward the impulses from our own primitive, reptilian, or snake like mind. This example involves trauma. As I've said in the cautions section (page 45), cathartic techniques, or any self-guided techniques, might not be sufficient with trauma.

Jason and Kevin are friends. Jason works as a herpetologist. He handles reptiles, including snakes, almost daily as part of his job. Kevin fears snakes. He can't bear to look at them. If a snake suddenly appears on television, he changes the channel as quickly as he can.

Jason and Kevin go on a hike in the woods. After turning a blind corner in the trail, Jason and Kevin simultaneously look to their right to see a timber rattlesnake lying on a rock about ten feet from them. Kevin instantly jumps like a gazelle and starts running further down the trail. It occurs to him there might be other snakes on the trail, so he stops. His heart pounds, and he has no idea what to do next.

Jason is very excited. It's rare to see a timber rattlesnake in the wild, especially a fat one that looks to be four feet long. Jason pulls out his camera and starts taking pictures. He bends down to get a better shot and moves a little closer. Jason is overconfident. He doesn't notice how close he is to the snake and that the snake doesn't have an easy escape route. The snake sinks its fangs into Jason's forearm and doesn't let go. The snake's fangs must have at least grazed a bone in Jason's arm because the pain is so intense that he almost faints.

From the way that Jason cries out, Kevin knows something is very wrong. Kevin cautiously walks back to Jason. He sees Jason holding the snake behind its head. Jason is trying to get the snake to let go of his arm but without success. Jason yells at Kevin to cut the snake with a knife. Kevin just stands frozen. Jason yells and curses at Kevin to cut the snake. Kevin somehow manages to cut the snake, starts to hyperventilate, and then vomits.

Jason starts to walk back to his car. Kevin finally pulls himself together and follows. Jason hopes the snake bit him defensively since that would mean it injected little to no venom. However, he feels dizzy and the area around the bite is swelling. Both are signs of venom. He tries to be as calm as possible but he knows he's feeling shock. He knows he might not survive the hour walk back to his car.

Jason woke up in the hospital and wondered how he got there. His left arm was very sore. Kevin had put Jason's left arm over his shoulder and mostly carried Jason to the car. Kevin is taller than Jason so Jason's left arm bore most of his weight. A doctor informed Jason there was little venom from the bite, and there shouldn't be any damage to his right arm. The bite did chip a bone in his arm, and he will need to wear a cast for at least a month.

All of that happened on Saturday. Now it's Monday. Jason keeps thinking over and over how his stupidity caused the destruction of a rare and incredible animal. Jason's boss told him to take as much time as he needs to recuperate. Jason's boss was talking about Jason's physical wounds. Jason now has a different problem. He feels traumatized. Now, he's not sure if he can ever return to work and handle another snake.

Thinking about it just makes him tremble. Jason realizes that he has to deal with his trauma or find another career.

Kevin feels disgusted with himself. His stupid fear might have cost the life of his friend. He's now determined to deal with his fear of snakes.

Let's say Jason and Kevin have read this book, and have practiced the techniques. Both know that they need to focus on their bodily sensations associated with snakes and their experience on the hike.

Jason starts imagining the snakes at his work. He has handled them thousands of times with comfort so maybe that will help. He soon realizes that his trauma, and sensations that go with it, are about the experience on the hike, but he's not sure he can experience that again even in his imagination. He tries the fly-on-the-wall technique (page 68). In his imagination, he puts himself in a tree where he can watch himself and the snake. By doing that, he can remain in the scene and watch himself do the stupid things he did. He remembers that behind the snake were steep rocks, and it couldn't escape. He understands the snake did what any snake would do. He can't blame it at all.

He starts to notice that he doesn't really have any discomfort with the snake, or that the snake bit him. He's confused. What else happened there? What did Kevin do? Kevin was worthless, at least at first, but that's not it either. Then he remembers starting to hike back to his car. He remembers feeling dizzy and ... Jason starts sobbing uncontrollably. He realizes that his trauma is from being sure he was going to die. He's never been that close to death before. He cries as long as he can, then goes back to focusing on his bodily sensations. Now he realizes how he's not at all prepared to consider his actual death. He realizes this is just the beginning of how he needs to consider the reality of death in every way he can. He needs to gain some comfort with just the fact that it's possible. Conversely, he also realizes that he should cherish life ever more. Jason feels great relief. He knows he can go back to work. He'll

feel as comfortable handling snakes as he ever has.
Handling snakes wasn't the problem.

Kevin uses pictures of snakes to stimulate his fear of snakes.
By focusing on his bodily sensations, he quickly gains
comfort with doing that. He then imagines the experience on
the hike. Much to his surprise, remembering the hike
doesn't bother him, but he stays with it for several minutes.
Then it occurs to him that maybe Jason would let him hang
around at his job. Maybe he could watch how Jason handles
snakes. He wonders why he hadn't thought of that before.
Maybe in time, he will feel like handling the snakes. For
whatever reason, that seemed like an exciting idea, and
Kevin felt a strong sense of relief.

GETTING A HANDLE ON EMOTIONS

Activated Emotion with No Understanding of Its Cause

When you feel hurt or angry, and you have no idea why, it
can be difficult to work with the cathartic techniques,
especially if the emotion is strong. Until you have some
understanding and comfort with the emotion, you can't
focus on anything. Getting a solid mental handle on a strong
emotion enables focusing on the sensations of the emotion.
As you gain comfort, you can move beyond mental handles
and focus primarily on bodily sensations.

Here's a list of some common handles. Hopefully, one of
these will fit what you're feeling and give you some idea
about what is bothering you. When you get a handle on an
emotion, look for another handle that fits the sensation even
better. For catharsis, the handle isn't important. Searching
for a handle--and the awareness of bodily sensations that
brings--is the important aspect of this technique. Looking for
an even better handle will bring your focus back to your
sensations.
  • Self. I'm awful because I can't accomplish what I
    think I should accomplish. No one likes me. I'm ugly.

81

I'm tired all the time and can barely do all that I need to do.

- Relationship (mother, father, spouse, friend). My mother is ignoring me. She never gave me the affection I need. My spouse doesn't respect or love me. My best friend doesn't really like me very much.
- Group (peer group, coworkers, a group of friends, the neighborhood association, and so on). They don't respect my opinions. They think I'm stupid. They don't like me. They're all stupid.
- Society at large (the general public, the shopping center, the country, and so on). I'm going to get fired. My job has no prestige. I'm a loser. Everyone is more successful than me.
- Existence. Everything is too much. I just want to sleep. Life isn't worth all the pain.

Any emotion can consume you for no apparent reason, and you can have no understanding of what the emotion is about. It could be depression, jealousy, feeling rejected, or feeling happy--all for no apparent reason. Anxiety about an emotion can be much greater when you don't understand where it came from--or when it will go away. Focusing on the bodily sensations associated with these kind of emotions can be easier because you don't have to imagine anything. The emotion and its sensations are very much present.

Focusing on the bodily sensations of an emotion will usually bring to mind an idea or mental interpretation of that emotion. If you're convinced a particular interpretation is helpful, take some time to ponder it, write it down, and so on. Keep looking for interpretations that feel more and more accurate. You'll be able to sense this in your body. By using exaggeration, you can find the boundaries of what feels accurate.

Here's a short example of using exaggeration. I'm feeling depressed and have no idea why. I shift my focus to my bodily sensations. The thought pops into my mind that I'll have to sell my car and get a roommate.

Maintaining my focus on bodily sensations, I begin to exaggerate these thoughts. I'll have to give up my home. My siblings won't take care of me, or if they do, it won't be for long. I'll end up begging on the streets of my hometown. People from high school might pity me and hand me a dollar. That would be very embarrassing.

My exaggeration causes me to see clearly that none of this is true. If I actually look for a better paying job, I might get one. And if not, a part-time job for a few months will get me out of debt. I find I'm feeling much better. What was I depressed about? Where's the job section of the newspaper?

Getting a Handle on Emotions by Asking, "If I were in a situation where this emotion or feeling fit, what would that situation be?"

Whenever I ask myself this, the answer always makes me feel better. It snaps me back to reality and brings back clarity.

Here's a personal example. While dating someone, I got very jealous. I got much more jealous than ever before and more than made any sense. Jealousy would just come over me for no apparent reason. I asked myself what situation I might be in where those feelings would fit or make sense. The answer: I'm three or four years old. I lose sight of my mother in a department store. I can't find her; I start to panic and cry. For a child, those feelings would be fitting and rational.

Answering that question somehow reminded me of the reality of my situation with the woman I was dating. I didn't really know what she did when I wasn't around. I didn't know her well enough to judge if she would lie to me or not. I saw the situation more clearly and realistically. I adjusted my heart accordingly. In that case, my jealousy didn't really lessen but I was comfortable with it. I figured there was a reason for it and it would reveal itself at some point. (The day after we broke up, she had dinner with her ex-boyfriend.

I think she was carrying a torch for him during our relations. Maybe I was picking that up in the ether. Hmmm.)

How did the memory of losing my mother in a department store clarify the situation with my girlfriend? Does it matter? This process updated my memes. The jealousy didn't go away but I didn't resist it any longer. I became fascinated with the jealousy. This is an example of how awareness alone causes the desired effect--catharsis. The ideas or emotions that occur during the process won't necessarily make sense, but they don't need to.

Emotion with a Fixed Definition of Its Cause

Having a fixed definition of your anxiety or emotions can get in the way of catharsis. It usually stops further exploration of your experience.

For example, let's say Sarah theorizes that she sometimes feels insecure or shy because she is the youngest in her family. Her siblings were always bigger and smarter, so she felt timid about saying anything at the dinner table. That created a habit of feeling shy with groups of people. She didn't talk much at the dinner table or in any group of people. That is her fixed idea about why she is shy.

Based on that insight, she starts talking freely. Being the youngest doesn't matter any longer. She is an adult. Her ideas are as valid as anyone's ideas. It's silly not to talk as freely as she wants. She tells her friends about her theory, and they agree with it wholeheartedly.

At first, Sarah's new approach is very exciting. She finally feels like she can express herself as much as she wants. Increasingly though, she notices that people seem annoyed with her. She struggles to think of reasons for that. She looks for another fixed idea that will explain why people react to her the way they do--but without success. She asks a close friend to help her. Her friend confesses that she says simple things as if they are profound or intelligent.

84

It occurs to Sarah that her mother would tell her how smart she was, even when her accomplishments were only average. That created a habit of stating simple ideas as if they were profound or intelligent. She then tries not to oversell her ideas but that also has consequences she doesn't like. She creates more and more theories to try to understand, but somehow they don't give her the peace she wants. She feels like she's going in circles.

Sarah doesn't realize that she is trying to make life's spontaneity and complexity fit her relatively simple fixed ideas. Her theories draw her attention away from her awareness of what is really happening. She's primarily using her thinking mind and not benefitting from her senses, or the capabilities of her primitive mind. If she used her full mind to build memes about how her feelings can help her, she wouldn't need to create theories about why she is the way she is.

Ask Yourself, "If this feeling lasted the rest of my life, could I live with it?"

For me, the answer to this, almost one hundred percent of the time is: Well sure, it's not that bad. This wakes me up from what I like to call an anxiety trance, or a strong and unnecessary fixation on anxiety. This question gives me some needed and realistic perspective. On rare occasions, when the answer is no, I usually realize I need to make some real changes in my life, or at least rethink some things.

IMAGINATION

? How can my imagination help me with _____?
? How can my imagination help me feel more comfortable?
Of course, there's no limit to imagination, but I think a good cathartic use of it is imagining something you want to accomplish. Say you want to get a better job or a better career, or perhaps you want to start your own business. Imagine any possible scene you might be in, and notice the

sensations that come up. If you feel discomfort, focus even more on the sensations associated with the situation. It might be the discomfort from a job interview, or the loneliness and responsibility of being your own boss and having people work for you.

You can also use imagination for something as simple as planning your day more effectively. I've found this remarkably powerful. Previously, I had no idea how much anxiety, even subtle anxiety, was stopping me from achieving simple goals. I realized how these anxieties turned into excuses for putting off work to the next day. I wasn't too tired to work; I was tired from anxiety. I get plenty of recreation, so I didn't need more. I needed relief from anxiety. Without anxiety, I've found I can bring the full power of my skills to any goal.

Contrasting Imagination With Reality

This technique is imagining something better for you, making it happen in your life, and being comfortable with all aspects of it. This technique also helps prevent you from inadvertently creating conflict or resistance toward your current sensations, emotions, or ideas.

For example, imagine what it would be like if you were as successful as you can be on your job. Focus on the bodily sensations of that. Everyone likes you, likes working with you, and you're promoted every year. But the more you focus on the sensations of that, the more likely you'll feel conflicted unpleasant sensations and emotions. That's because you've created a conflict between the new imagined ideas and what you currently feel is true. You're not promoted every year, so thinking you are just seems contradictory and phony.
? How can my past feelings help with new ideas or feelings?

Work with your current sensations about your job. Focus on the bodily sensations of those ideas and emotions to gain comfort with them. Then go back to imagining that you're successful. Is there any anxiety about seeing you as a complete success? Are there any ideas or feelings that you don't deserve success? Maybe you automatically think you're too stupid to achieve the success you can imagine. If so, fully engage the bodily sensations of those ideas or feelings.

Even though your thinking mind can have problems with contradictory ideas, there's no reason you can't have a catharsis with the sensations of contradictory ideas. When your sensations are comfortable, the thinking mind can easily accept contradictory ideas. You become comfortable and free to use whatever ideas you choose. Out of habit, your thinking mind might bring up how worthless and stupid you are to think you'll ever be a success. Because you now associate comfort with that idea, you can smile and feel glad that those ideas won't bother you any longer.

WORKING WITH SUBTLE MEMES

Sometimes you don't have any significant anxiety and no pressing issues come to mind. That's when you can just take inventory of your body, thoughts, or subtle emotions. See what's there. Let it take you wherever it wants to go. Just have fun.

Sometimes you can find a sensation in your body that doesn't seem to be associated with anything. It's just there. You've had autonomic sensations like hunger and digestion all of your life. You've had them before you had language or the ability to associate any thoughts to them. If there is no strong anxiety associated with something like hunger or digestion, you're not likely to have associated thoughts or emotions. The sensation is just there.

You might notice mild tension that easily relaxes just by giving it attention. Mild tension, subtle muscle tension, or subtle nervous tension can be most interesting. Focusing attention on those can release lifelong tension that has drained your energy all of your life. Can you find subtle fear or aggression even though you generally feel fine? Combining this focus with CONNECTED BREATHING (see page 115) can create a deep and powerful catharsis.

Here's something of a warning. Especially at first, doing this can make you very sleepy. Focusing awareness on subtle sensations can seem like deep uncharted territory. Getting sleepy might be a defense against experience you're not ready to bring to your awareness. Or, focusing on subtle sensations might just be relaxing. Either way, you might want to do this when you don't have any responsibilities for the rest of the day, and you can catch up on sleep.

Working with subtle memes is only feasible if you have little anxiety and your thinking mind is calm. If a thought or emotion keeps popping into your awareness, you should probably shift your focus to the associated sensations of that, rather than risk creating conflict with thoughts or emotions that need attention.

MAKING BODILY SENSATIONS MORE OBVIOUS

To make bodily sensations more obvious, try this: flex, stretch, or tense any muscle, hold the muscle in that position for as long as you like, then relax it. Move a little, stretch, contract and relax muscles, feel more or less tension in general or in any part of your body; feel the chair, the bedding, or whatever surface you're on. Notice your position, posture, or your sense of balance. Change your posture slightly. Ask yourself, if you could feel less tension and feel more relaxed, how would you know this? What exactly could be less tense?

Awareness Using Touching, Rubbing, or Tapping

This exercise is pressing (tapping, or rubbing if you prefer) on various parts of your body with your fingertips. Press for as long as you feel you need or want to press. You can have someone else do the pressing but I suggest you do it by yourself at first. Doing this alone would be best before adding the emotional responses that come with another person touching you.

While touching, focus on the following:
- Notice how other parts of your body seem to react to the part of your body you touch.
- Other than where you're pressing, what is the most dominant sensation? Is it connected to where you're touching?
- Are your thoughts or emotions coming from your touch, or are they coming from your usual mental chitchat?
- Can you associate or connect the sensation from your touch to anything in the room, a block away, a thousand miles away?
- Move your eyes while touching. Look to your left side, look up and to the left, up and forward, up and to the right, to the right side, down and to the right, down forward, down to the left, straight ahead, and so on. Hold each gaze long enough to ponder the previous questions or longer if desired. This eye movement usually activates different parts of your brain and creates an association with the characteristics of each part.
- Let the sensations of pressing on a body part suggest the next body part to explore.

I think it's important that you don't make this exercise (or any exercise) routine. If you know the acupressure points or the body meridians, I suggest you don't favor them or assume using them is better than any other part of your body. Keep search mode (page 25) alive and let yourself be surprised. Pressing on one part of your body could seem uneventful on one day. On another day, the same spot could send waves of sensation throughout your entire body.

Here is an example sequence. You don't need to follow this feet-to-head sequence. Your sequence can be as random as you want. However, I think a sequence that includes most areas of your body is best.

- The bottom of your feet (for hard to reach places, you can use massage tools, or anything that works like tennis balls, golf balls, etc.)
- press where the top of your foot meets the ankle
- shins just above your feet
- calves
- just below your knees.
- behind your knees
- thighs just above the knees.
- the crease where your legs meet your stomach between your hip and pubis
- the stomach
- various parts of the chest
- various parts of the back, lower, middle, upper, around the shoulder blades (put a couple of tennis balls or something similar between your back and the back of a chair)
- front of the neck.
- where your shoulder meets your neck
- The base of the skull and back of the neck
- under the ears and on the back of the jaw bone
- under or around your eyes
- forehead
- top of your head

Usually with massage or yoga, you get the most benefit if you reach the point just before physical pain. However, soft pressure can work as well as hard pressure for bringing awareness to your body and for catharsis. Try both and see for yourself. If you have long fingernails and you want to press hard, use an appropriate tool such as a pencil or most anything lying around the house. Even though I've listed tapping and rubbing as a technique, I haven't used them much. So far, I find both too distracting. Maybe I will find them useful in the future.

Other cathartic processes can be added to this sequence of pressing on your body. I've found these most powerful:
- connected breathing (page 115)
- a mantra (page 119)

MAKING NERVOUS SYSTEM SENSATIONS MORE OBVIOUS

Anxiety mostly affects and is associated with your sympathetic nervous system (see, THE AUTONOMIC NERVOUS SYSTEM, page 161). Anxiety can affect your breathing, muscle tension, and heart rate. Here are a few ways to make the subtle sensations of your nervous system more pronounced and obvious. Keep in mind, any of these focuses could also make muscle tension or emotions more intense. Feel free to change your focus to muscle tension or an emotion and return to focusing on your nervous system later.

Change Your Breathing

Try breathing faster, deeper, slower, or more shallow. Try emptying your lungs and holding your exhale for a few seconds. Even a minor change can draw attention toward your breath. A big change can be distracting, difficult to maintain, and draw attention away from your breath. See, CONNECTED BREATHING, page 115 for an in-depth look at this method.

Let Your Breathing Do What It Wants

This technique is based on the premise that you usually control your breathing to some degree. Some people agree with that and some don't. Possibly the people who disagree with it don't control their breathing, or they're just not aware of it; I'm not sure. But if you do agree that sometimes you control your breathing, I think you'll find this technique very powerful.

It works like this: Focus on your breathing and try to get a sense of what it wants to do or is inclined to do. For example, try exhaling and not inhaling until you're sure you want to. What feels more natural--to push on your exhale, or to hold back on it? How deep or shallow of an inhale feels the most natural? Is your inhale constrained, or free? If it's constrained, let it be constrained. What attitude or emotion

91

would you assign to your breathing? Is it angry, sad, or tired? Is it crying?

When I first tried this, I tended to pause after my exhale, and I was reluctant to inhale. Possibly, I had some low-level depression that I hadn't noticed before. I kept focusing. Soon, my breathing spontaneously and naturally evened out and I felt much better.

I found doing this while sitting on a park bench with many people around to be very beneficial. It was like focusing on sensations in real time and real life, not just in my imagination. It's always good to work with discomfort or anxiety in real life situations if you can. In the past, I've tended to be slightly agoraphobic, yet the physical comfort I achieved in public with this breathing method has lasted, and I don't notice that particular phobia any longer.

One caution: not controlling your breathing has the benefit of revealing your general physical and emotional state. If you're very anxious, however, your breath could speed up to the point of hyperventilation. If this happens, you should probably control it enough to keep it at a manageable and relaxed level.

Feeling Your Heartbeat

You might be able to feel your heartbeat, especially if you're tense, angry, or just drank a cup of coffee. You can also feel a sense of pressure, or lack of pressure, extending from your heart up through your head. Can you feel your temples move every time your heart beats? Even if you can't feel your heartbeat in detail, you can usually get a sense of the pressure or movement throughout your body that comes from its movement.

One way to make your heartbeat more obvious, is to sit in a chair with your back straight. While keeping your back straight, lean forward a few inches or until your nose is over your mid thigh. This should enhance the sensation of your heart beating.

Why try to feel your heartbeat? It's not clear that the cardiac muscle (your heart), like other muscles, can habitually hold unnecessary tension. If it does, imagine the pervasive positive effect of permanently relaxing that tension. At very least, awareness of your heart will expose tensions that affect your heart. It can also be very relaxing.

Fight-or-Flight Response

Look for sensations that seem to urge you to fight or to flee, or that seem connected with anger or fear. It seems the fight-or-flight response pervades many of our sensations and muscles, and even our posture. Perhaps you know someone who seems like they're always fighting the world, and someone else who seems afraid of the world. You might even have one of these attitudes yourself--or even both at the same time.

I'm not saying the fight-or-flight response is bad. After all, it's basic to how we function, and probably saves our lives more times than we know. It's only when such responses are both unnecessary and habitual that they drain our energy. Bringing awareness to bodily sensations that contain these unnecessary responses can help break their habitual nature.

Stress While Concentrating

Try to concentrate on something that overwhelms your ability to concentrate. For example, count down from one thousand. If that is too easy, use the ticking of a clock to count down from one thousand, and think of the next number every second. Think of a three-syllable word that starts with A, then Z, and continue with that pattern: B and Y, C and X, D and W, and so on.

The point of this exercise is to activate any resistance you have toward the stress you feel when concentrating on something that is overwhelming. By focusing on that resistance, you can increase your comfort with concentration, and your ability to concentrate.

WORKING WITH HUNGER

This section has nothing to do with going on a diet. The techniques are only for creating comfort with hunger impulses. But, of course, when you're comfortable with hunger impulses, you can more easily choose what to eat and when to eat it. You'll no longer have nagging hunger impulses that you'll fight or resist.

This section is something of a template for focusing on autonomic sensations in general, and hunger in this particular case. This template might or might not work for you, but it could help point you toward what could work for you. You'll probably need the template plus your own judgment and instinct to discover what will work for you. Since hunger is a deeply ingrained autonomic sensation, you might not feel you're having success with this template unless you've practiced the cathartic techniques for several months. But I could be wrong.

Hunger changes constantly throughout the day. Have you ever planned to eat little, and before the day is over, you've talked yourself into eating food you didn't need? I can plan to feel a particular hunger sensation all day, but five minutes later I have a different hunger sensation and I have to start over. However, once you realize and accept that's the nature of hunger, or any autonomic impulse, you won't feel frustrated. Autonomic impulses are something you live with. They aren't resolved or fixed. Trying to control an autonomic impulse is foolhardy. You'll always fail. The only practical option is to use and engage impulses. If you could take a pill to "control" or "fix" your appetite, it would necessarily disrupt your appetite and your autonomic nervous system. Destructive side effects couldn't be avoided.

Do skinny people have less of an appetite than overweight people, or do they just have a different relationship to their appetite? Possibly, they have less resistance to their hunger impulses so they don't feel anxious and then eat to relieve their anxiety.

Ask thin people how they react to food cravings during the day. I think you will generally find they just think about how good their next planned meal will be. Generally, they grew up eating meals on a schedule. They don't usually eat between meals.

Or you might find others who have a strong sense of when they are truly hungry physically. The idea of eating when they don't feel physically hungry would be weird to them.

I don't know the answer to any of these questions. Asking people with different body types how they experience hunger throughout the day, can be interesting. Ask different types of people how they would enjoy eating two pounds of pasta in five minutes, and note the wide range of reactions.

The primary issue with hunger, I think, is the thinking mind generates thoughts based in the past or future and the primitive mind has no sense of time. You promise yourself you'll eat less tomorrow. Your primitive mind hears that thought as an attack on its purpose. Your primal hunger function never wants to hear that you intend to eat less. Denied hunger will scream like a baby until it gets its way (see, HOW THE REPTILIAN, MAMMALIAN, AND THINKING MINDS INTERACT AND AFFECT EACH OTHER, page 168). So, trying to deal with hunger (or any autonomic response) with just the thinking mind usually creates conflict and frustration. An integrated full mind approach is needed. These techniques activate as many parts of the mind as possible via feelings, association, impulses, and extremes.

? How can I feel more comfortable with my hunger?
Questions like this will greatly help direct your attention toward your visceral sensations of hunger. That attention can create comfort with any sensation. Keep in mind that using a question is just a way to direct your attention. If you

can focus directly on sensations without using a question, that is usually more powerful.

Engage Hunger Sensations Using Association

? How does my hunger comfortably fit with all that is happening?
When you feel hungry, associate those feelings with anything or anyone in your current surroundings. Do that for as long as needed or as long as you want. Even if you do this for fifteen seconds daily, then eat what you usually do, you can gain much comfort and options with hunger sensations.

Engage Impulses or Cravings for Food

? How can I feel comfortable indulging my cravings?
When you feel an impulse or craving for food, indulge it with your imagination (see, ENGAGING AND INDULGING IMPULSES, page 63). Usually, I indulge the impulse, then I use my imagination to indulge what I think I should eat. That usually satisfies the original impulse. Then I can get back to focusing on whatever I was doing and eat what I want to eat later.

If you decide to eat what you're craving, focus in detail as fully as you can on all the sensations of doing that. In other words, try to enjoy it more than you usually do.

Hunger As a Genetic Memory

Compare the following scenario with your current everyday experience. Are there any similarities between your experience, and living in a tribe?

Imagine you live with a tribe. Feeling hunger is a constant panic inducing reminder that you might never find enough food. When you have food, you want to eat as much as possible because you're not sure when you'll find more food.

You and your tribe think about food most of the time. How can we get more? How can we preserve it? How can we prepare it? If the tribe thinks you're not doing enough to obtain food, or you're eating more than your share, they might punish or beat you.

Sometimes, food is plentiful. The tribe celebrates with festive dance. Everyone is happy and eating much food prepared in many different ways.

Engage the Emotions of Hunger

? How can my emotions that are associated with hunger, help me?
Focus on the bodily sensations of any emotion associated with hunger. Some of the more common emotions are:

- I'm worthless and weak because I have these cravings and because I usually give into them. After I give into them, I feel good, and then I feel ever more worthless and weak.
- I'll die or get sick if I don't eat enough. (How true is that? What is enough nutrition and what do you need to eat to get enough?)
- If you use food to relieve stress, how will you relieve stress if you change your diet?
- If you don't eat all of your mothers cooking, and enjoy it the way you always have, she'll feel hurt.
- While dining with friends, you want to eat healthy food but your friends eat food that's not so healthy-- food you love. Their food is too tempting. Or, you do eat healthily and cause anxiety in your friends. Since you're eating a healthy and sensible meal, they feel like gluttons.

Using Extremes

You eat as much as you want of anything you want. Because of that, you become obese but you don't care. You've decided that being obese is better than trying to deny the sensations of being hungry. You're going to enjoy your life.

Conversely, you maintain a strict diet that limits your daily intake of calories. You take pride that you can deal with sensations of feeling hungry no matter how strong the sensations might be. You know all the places you can go to get low calorie food. You know exactly what to say when someone comments on how little you eat or that maybe you're too thin.

This is primarily a mental exercise. Its purpose is to gain more comfort with either extreme, and by consequence, everything between those extremes.

CATHARSIS WITH PERSISTENT AUTONOMIC SENSATIONS

Many elements of mind are short-lived or change over time. Some memories, emotions, and things we imagine fade away and never return to awareness. We resolve troubling emotions and memories that never enter awareness again in any noticeable way. Beliefs, views, and generalizations about anything usually change over time whether you notice it or not.

Autonomic bodily functions, and any associated sensations, never go away. You will always experience them to some degree. Some of these are: the fight-or-flight response, hunger, digestion, ingestion, elimination, sleep, rejuvenation, exhaustion, sexual desire. Discomfort or anxiety with any of these experiences can torture you daily.

Achieving catharsis with autonomic sensations can be more complex and take more time because of the following factors.

- Skill. The ability to be aware of bodily sensations (interoception) is a skill. At first, you might not have enough skill to deal effectively with hunger or other autonomic bodily sensations (It took me about two months once I started with hunger). It takes skill to recognize when you're resisting an autonomic bodily sensation. Resistance to autonomic bodily sensations can be very subtle.

- Like a spontaneous emotion, any autonomic sensation is usually involuntary and just happens. You don't need to remember or imagine anything. Using your mind to stimulate an autonomic response can be difficult and even delusional. It's usually best to work with autonomic responses as they happen.
- Autonomic bodily sensations might have no conscious mental representation and seem hidden. You've had these sensations since birth if not before. You started to experience them before you had language or the ability to define them mentally. Saying you're accustomed to them is putting it mildly. Frequently, you only become aware of them from a drastic physical change like illness, irregular sleep patterns, or a major change in diet.
- If you do have a significant catharsis with autonomic sensations, your sense-of-self can become disoriented. You won't feel like yourself. Your sense-of-self is strongly tied to those familiar sensations. It's easy to want to feel like you did before a catharsis, even though you had more stress. In that sense, it's good to work with autonomic sensations a little at a time instead of trying to have a catharsis all at once. Of course, that's a matter for your best judgment.
- Emotions associated with autonomic sensations can be extensive and conflicting. Some people want to tell you about the best diet and how you could eat better. Then if you order a salad, other people look at you like you're being rude and not joining the party. That's just one of the many ways that food cravings can be a major source of anxiety.
- Frustration. You feel like it's taking too long. You feel like you're not resisting anything but you're not getting the results you expect.

Here are some general approaches for working with autonomic sensations. As always, the primary goal is to find resistance or stress, and focus on the sensations of either. In the previous section, WORKING WITH HUNGER, page 94,

I describe a more detailed approach using hunger as an example. You could use that as a template for more detailed work with the following.

- The fight-or-flight response. Use a memory or something imagined to stimulate either the fight-or-flight response.
- Digestion. Notice how your heart beats faster and stronger after a large meal. Focus on the sensation of food in your stomach. See how long you can sense it after a meal.
- Ingestion. Play with your food before eating it. Eat very very slowly being mindful of everything you can about eating. Chew forever. Conversely, gulp it down. Eat very fast. Try to be as unconscious as you can about eating.
- Elimination. In your imagination, urinate and defecate everywhere you can think of. Conversely, in your imagination, urinate and defecate on a very strict schedule. Never let anyone know that you did either. Alter your diet so you can be sure that you can stick to the schedule. Imagine how angry your mother was when she tried to potty train you and you couldn't do it right. Conversely, imagine your mother in no way felt stress with your potty training. Have you ever felt embarrassed by farting at the wrong time or the wrong place?
- Sleep or exhaustion. What do you feel as soon as you wake up? Does it feel like you slept well? If not, ponder any changes you could make. Stay awake all night, or just very late, and focus in detail on your sensations.
- Rejuvenation. I think the awareness by touch technique is best for rejuvenation and its associated sensations (see, Awareness Using Touching, Rubbing, or Tapping, page 88). In general, your ability to rejuvenate, heal and relax, also activates when you're exhausted. Also see Indulging Depression - Intentional Disassociation, page 59.
- Sexual desire. Masturbate but don't have an orgasm. As you can probably imagine, focusing on your bodily sensations while masturbating can be intense, very

emotional and create much resistance and impatience. Don't be surprised or ashamed if you can't do this at first. However, with success, the effects of this focus can be powerful. Using extremes, spend at least ten minutes imagining the following. Imagine you have a harem. Imagine eight people are simultaneously massaging you. You're having sex with the most beautiful people you can imagine. For the other extreme, at least once a day, someone feels the need to tell you how unbelievably ugly you are. They give you advice on plastic surgery. They try to tell you how to carry yourself so you don't look awkward and dorky. The last time you asked someone for a date, they were so appalled they just walked away. Remember an embarrassing time as a child. For example, when Aaron was about four years old, his penis fell out of his pajamas in front of his older sister and her friends. They all laughed until Aaron ran to his room crying. Or, as a pubescent girl, you felt confused and uncomfortable about the way boys started leering at your body.

Other types of persistent experience are mental viewpoints or generalizations (see, GENERALIZATIONS, page 122) that are usually unavoidable. For example, unless you're a hermit, you have an ingrained viewpoint about people that occurs daily since you see people daily.

You might see people as something to fear and that makes you shy. Or you might see people as very connected to you and they always want to hear anything you want to talk about--or anything between those two. Personally, when I started focusing on my bodily sensations associated with people in general, I started realizing how much ingrained fear I had. That type of fear has a flip side of me being aloof and being unaware when people are being nice to me. Those were unsettling things to realize about myself but I'm glad I did.

ENGAGING BODILY SENSATIONS ABOUT OTHER PEOPLE

? How can my reactions to others help me?

The following techniques focus on bodily sensations associated with other people, or seem to be associated with other people. The sensations can be from being with other people, or imagining being with people.

When you gain comfort with your bodily sensations, any interaction is easier. Of course, this doesn't take the place of other social skills such as conflict resolution, expressing emotion, or being a good listener. These techniques help you feel comfortable in your own body when you're with others. That, in itself, can greatly reduce the need for conflict resolution and enhance your general connection to others.

These focuses didn't occur to me until I had practiced cathartic techniques for over a year. Just when I thought I had covered every resistance I had, I tried this and almost felt overwhelmed by it. These focuses exposed layer after layer of seemingly primal fear, anger, and general discomfort I've always felt about other people. After a couple of days, it occurred to me to start associating those bodily sensations to my surroundings and other people. I then experienced one of the most intense cathartic changes I've ever experienced. So, possibly, this focus is advanced. You might not be able to do it if you're not experienced with the techniques. However, there's no way I can know that for sure.

Bodily sensations related to other people are not technically the same as an autonomic sensation like hunger. However, like hunger, they can seem deeply ingrained and pervasive in every part of your psyche. You would probably need to use many different cathartic techniques like association, engaging impulses, engaging emotions, extremes, and genetic memory to illuminate your sensations about people and any ingrained resistance you have. See the template for using a full range of techniques, described in the section: WORKING WITH HUNGER, page 94.

I was surprised at how much resistance I had toward other people. Most of my life, I've exhausted myself thinking about ways to compensate for my discomfort with others. I constantly worried about how I can please others. What can I do, and say, when I'm with other people that would change their reaction to me. If only people liked me more, if only I were more popular, I would feel more comfortable.

Now I realize that I only need to accept those feelings and find ways to use them. I didn't need to analyze them, figure them out, or hide them from others. Possibly my discomfort was due to primal genetic memories. Maybe I copied those feelings from one or both of my parents and they copied them from their parents. However, those speculations don't matter. The feelings are there and they are part of me. I can react to them or not. I can look for how they could be useful or not. Now, since I'm not resisting those sensations, they don't draw my attention inward and get in the way of engaging other people.

I remember a cartoon character (Jiminy Cricket I think) singing, "just act naturally." That always sounded like good advice but I was never sure of what it meant exactly. I didn't know how to act naturally so it didn't help. Now I feel like I do know how to act naturally. By looking for ways to connect my spontaneous feelings to others, I can truly be myself.

Associating My Feelings With Others

? How can all my feelings fit or work with another's feelings?
Take note of all your sensations, tensions, and reactions to others. As best as you can, take note of another person's sensations, tensions, and reactions to you.

Do you feel that any of your sensations can't mingle with another person's sensations or behavior? If so, ask yourself how feelings that seem to conflict, can coexist and work together. Can you find more ways that your sensations can mingle or combine with another person?

To be clear, I'm only referring to bodily sensations, and any resistance you might have to experiencing your sensations fully. The specific interaction between you and another person doesn't matter. You could be having a heart-to-heart conversation or a fist fight. However, if you have no resistance toward your sensations, and theirs, you'll likely not fight.

Here's a list of general association patterns you might have or you might see in others. As an exercise, determine which patterns you have, try to do the opposite, and then note the physical sensations you have. For example, if you usually study people and don't talk very much, try to talk as much as you can. By finding discomfort with behavior patterns you don't usually have, you can gain options or even new abilities you can use when relating to others.

This exercise centers on how the listed behaviors affect your attention. Are you comfortable focusing attention or do you usually divert your attention? Can you focus indefinitely or do you get more uncomfortable the longer you hold your attention on a specific interpersonal interaction listed below?

It's certainly not a complete list. If your reaction isn't listed, the listed reactions can help you think of what your reaction is. This exercise works best when you are completely honest with yourself. It also works best if you imagine a scene where the interaction has happened or could happen, and you focus on sensory details of the scene, that is--sights, sounds, skin sensations, tastes, and so on.

Emotion
- If someone is upset, angry, or depressed, do you try to comfort them? Or do you get uncomfortable and want them to talk about something else?

- Are you completely comfortable no matter how happy another person is? Or is there a point when it gets uncomfortable?
- Do you like compliments or are you uncomfortable with them?
- When someone is upset, do you usually think it has something to do with you? Or does that not occur to you?
- If someone gets mad do you feel you need to fix it? Do you blame yourself?
- Do you try to be up and positive when you sense discomfort?

Ego, will
- Do you frequently feel that others don't focus on you enough?
- Boundaries. Do you assume people won't cross your boundaries? Then do you sometimes feel angry because you realize they have been crossing your boundaries?
- Are you constantly on guard? Do you analyze everything anyone says or does to see if they are in some way offending you?
- Do you frequently struggle to get your way?
- Do you usually do what others want you to do, but sometimes feel angry that no one cares about what you want?
- Do you feel you end up leading whatever group you're in whether you want to or not?
- Do you usually talk more than others?
- Do you usually listen to others and study them?
- Do you always feel heard, listened to, respected?
- Are you ever a braggart or name dropper?
- Do you ever mirror or imitate others' behavior?
- Do you try to say and do what you think others will like?
- Do you feel uncomfortable if you are not the center of attention, or if you are?

Thoughts
- Do you love to argue your beliefs?

- Do you rarely admit you're wrong?
- Do you love to gossip?
- Which of these do you believe more, and do you see how they affect your relations with others?
  - Ideas, belief, and knowledge can solve all problems.
  - Knowledge is only a tool and a very limited tool. Any idea is only an inaccurate symbol of what is real and has no reality itself.

Physical responses
- Where is your comfort zone? How close is too close?
- Do you frequently move your body and fidget, or do you sit still?
- Do you have a nervous laugh or giggle? Do you frequently laugh when nothing is funny?

I'm not at all putting a value judgment on any of those interactions. These exercises are only for increasing awareness and physical comfort. More awareness and comfort usually resolve nervous habits and insecurity, even if you don't try to resolve them. Increased awareness of these interactions can help you react to them with more skill and satisfaction.

I felt I most needed to work with boundaries. I needed to check mine much more frequently. I usually don't, and then feel like people are taking advantage of me, whether they are or not. The biggest block to that practice was the idea that I shouldn't need to always be on guard. I finally realized being on guard enriches my interactions with others. By being clearer about my reactions and boundaries, people have more to relate to. Think of a person who always tries to do whatever you want and how boring that can be.

Extremes

Try to imagine both extremes as fully as you can. Try to use as many sensory details as you can (sights, sounds, smells, feelings on your skin, and so on).

- Everyone usually ignores you. If you draw attention to yourself, people will abuse you and make fun of you. Everyone makes you run errands for them.
- Conversely, you're invited to all parties and events. People constantly tell you how great you are. Everyone wants to be with you and listen to anything you want to say.

Old or Genetic Memory

Do any of the following scenarios fit your experience? See, GENETIC MEMORY, page 74, if you haven't already.

Are you experiencing other people through a filter of genetic memory? Are you reacting as if you fear your tribe might shun you and make you fend for yourself in the wilderness? Do you feel you're losing status with the tribe? Maybe a peer does a task better than you and gets more attention and appreciation from the whole tribe. A potential spouse rejects you and the whole tribe laughs at you.

Others are watching you but they pretend they are not watching you. They don't let you catch their looking at you. They wait for you to do something wrong so they can report you to the chief or elders.

Take any fear or aggression you feel when you are with other people and exaggerate it. If the fear or aggression were appropriate in a tribal situation, what situation would it be? Are those feelings based in anything that is real and happening to you in your current life and if so, to what degree?

Planning to Fear Others

Whatever fears or anxieties you have toward others, plan to feel them (see, Planning to Feel Anxiety All Day, page 56). Plan to look for how others wish you harm. Look for signs of bad intentions in everything they say and do. Plan to be as paranoid and as suspicious as you can be. The more you focus on the bodily sensations of those thoughts, and gain comfort with them, the more you can clearly see how people are really treating you.

Boundaries

Focus on the sensations caused by the following questions.

How close do you let others get to you, literally and figuratively? What would you feel if other people got much closer? Do you want people to get closer?

Do you cross others' boundaries or could you get closer without crossing their boundaries? Do you ever ask them? Do you talk much more than other people? Do you interrupt others when they are talking? What would you feel if you drastically changed that?

Do you talk much less than others? What would you feel if you drastically changed that? Do people frequently interrupt you? What would you feel if you insisted that they don't interrupt you?

Do you study others at all? If you don't, can you? What sensations would you have if you kept looking for something you haven't seen before in others? What reaction would others have if you studied them? Would they like it? Would you like it if others studied you?
? What have I never seen about this person?

Do you have a strong fear of people disliking you? If so, can you focus on the bodily sensations of that? Are you too suspicious? Do you think most people will take advantage of you if you give them a chance? If so, can you focus on the bodily sensations of that?

ANXIETY ABOUT AN UPCOMING EVENT

This is an example of gaining comfort with an upcoming event. Samantha will play for her graduate piano recital tomorrow. She feels very nervous. She's afraid her hands will shake and she'll play badly. Her grades have been good so far, but if she doesn't play well tomorrow it could ruin her career. She fears her entire life could be ruined.

Samantha sits, closes her eyes, and focuses on the tension in her body. She imagines sitting at the piano on stage. She sees everyone in the audience blankly looking at her. She notices her breathing speed up and her chest getting tight. She looks for more details in these sensations.

After thirty seconds or so, she notices she wants to cry. She imagines letting herself cry in front of the audience. As she does, she scans her body for any changes in her sensations. She feels these sensations as much as she can. She imagines the audience can empathize with her and feel exactly what she feels. Her breathing becomes easier. She feels some relaxation in her breathing and in her upper body. Now she focuses on these new sensations. It never occurred to her that weeping could be relaxing. Soon, she begins to laugh. She sees humor in weeping in front of her recital audience. She continues to look for more detail in her bodily sensations.

She notices that she feels anger toward the audience. Who are they to judge me? Are they so perfect? In her imagination, she begins to look around the room. Because she has done cathartic processing before, she knows that her anxiety has given way to curiosity. Clarity is starting to replace her blindness caused by fear and resistance. Who will actually be there? Of course, the professors will be there. Judging her is their job. All of them are reasonable people, except Professor Prendergast, but Samantha feels she might have finally gotten on his good side. Her friends will be there too. Would they disown her if she played badly? They probably wouldn't. In her imagination, Samantha is starting to feel present and physically comfortable in the recital hall. She feels good, but she knows she hasn't had a catharsis yet.

She looks around the imaginary recital hall some more. She notices she isn't so anxious. She starts imagining how she will deal with all the physical aspects of her performance. She looks for even more detail in her bodily sensations. She imagines how she will walk out on stage, sit at the piano, play the songs, and stand up to take a bow.

She wonders how she can connect her bodily sensations with those of the audience. It occurs to her that she can play her songs so they physically connect to every person listening to her. Her hands and fingers can massage the piano keys and project the sound into the body of everyone in the audience. She can make them feel the music. With this thought, her entire body relaxes and comfort washes over her. Samantha has a catharsis. Eager anticipation replaces her fear and anxiety. She immediately goes to her piano to rehearse the music. She imagines how to make it physically enjoyable to her listeners.

To be clear, Samantha's primary focus was to put her awareness on her bodily sensations. Note that although she started to relax early in her focus, she didn't stop her process. She experienced thoughts and emotions that seemed to arise out of her bodily sensations, but these thoughts and emotions didn't represent a goal or even a stopping point. Her goal was simply to focus on her sensations. She didn't stop when she experienced interesting thoughts or revelations, nor when she began experiencing pleasant emotions; nor even when she realized how good and relaxed she felt. She stopped only after she experienced a perceptual shift. In other words, she stopped only when her anticipated experience of the recital became fully comfortable.

While imagining her recital, her body relaxed simply because she focused attention on her sensations. Her thinking mind followed along and generated ideas that corresponded to feeling physically comfortable. Her emotions began to match her physical comfort and ideas. Then she reached a tipping point where her comfort was greater than her discomfort.

She could experience being fully present and engaged at her recital. Samantha had a catharsis.

SENSATIONS OF RECENT EVENTS

You're upset or angry about last night or any recent event. So and so was a jerk; they made you look stupid. If only you had said this or that. Your mind goes round and round, dwelling on the last night's events and wishing they had gone another way.

Instead of that, or in addition, keep any detail in mind about last night and focus on your bodily sensations until you feel comfortable with them and achieve a catharsis. You'll likely see the recent events in a more workable light.
? How could I have used my feelings last night?

CREATING IMPULSES

This technique is for adding new impulses to existing ones. The title of this section could be something like, "Changing or Replacing Unwanted Impulses." That might be how we usually approach unwanted impulses, but that wouldn't be in keeping with a cathartic approach. Trying to change an impulse, or not wanting an impulse, usually creates inner conflict.

Without experience with the techniques listed so far (particularly the association technique, page 47), this technique can easily create resistance or repression. You might need to remind yourself that you're trying to add impulses rather than change your existing impulses.
? How can my current desires help create new ones?

With this technique, you imagine scenes using elements of your senses that can be seen, heard, felt, tasted, or smelled. I'm sure there are many more senses than those five, but describing them concretely can be tricky. For example, the scope or range of space is how much space you perceive at once. Sometimes you might feel like you can take in an entire room all at once, or the entire sky. Other times, comprehending a small object three feet in front of you seems difficult. As another example, your sense of time can make an event seem like it's dragging or taking too long. Conversely, you can feel annoyed that something happened too fast.

The basic steps of this technique are as follows:
- Pick a scene that would activate an existing impulse. The scene can be from your imagination or your current experience. Fully indulge the physical sensations of this scene. Note when your sensations change even slightly.
- Pick a scene where your new impulse would fit. The scene can be the opposite of your current experience or slightly different. Your primitive mind doesn't know or care about opposites or contradiction. Associate your current bodily sensations with that scene. Don't try to change your sensations. Fully indulge the physical sensations of this scene. Note when your sensations change even slightly.
- From the previous two steps, does your primitive mind feel attacked? Do you sense conflict? If so, go back to your existing impulse. Or try to imagine your existing impulse and the new impulse together at the same time.
- Repeat until you don't sense conflict or for as long as desired.

? How can the details of my current habit help me remember the details of the new habit?

Let's use hunger as an example. My goal is to add an impulsive desire for protein drinks to the impulses I usually have when I'm hungry.

First, I imagine in detail the eggs and cheese I usually eat. The details include:
- the medium size cast iron skillet
- I usually forget to keep my garbage can open and need to open it for every eggshell

- some form of expensive cheese mixed in or on the eggs
- I sometimes scramble them, or fry two eggs--over medium--and put them on toast
- I time the toast, eggs and coffee so they're done at the same time

Second, I focus on the details of the protein drink that include:
- the large black two pound container
- the font on the container looks like a mix between Courier and Helvetica
- how I have to reach for the container since it's on a high shelf, (I should probably put it on a lower shelf)
- how I need to remember to fill my glass halfway before putting in a scoop of powder so it mixes easier
- then more water
- then using my mixer with only one beater and mixing the drink in the glass and so on.

With that, I have added an option. When I get the impulse to make eggs, I'll also get an impulse for a protein drink. I don't detect any adverse response from my primitive mind about the protein drink option.

Let's use shyness as another example. You want to ask Regina out for a date but your current thoughts and feelings are: Regina is out of my league and she knows it. There's no possibility that she would find me attractive. That idea wouldn't enter her mind. If I mentioned it, she would feel confused and uncomfortable. She would scramble for something to say. She would have trouble looking at me. Then I would get what I dread the most, a polite rejection.

Conversely, Regina very much wants you to ask her out on a date. She has for a long time. She thinks you're the greatest thing since butter. When you ask her out, she'll be nervous but she'll be so happy you did.

That would be the start of this technique. From there, you would need to add much more sensory detail like: the visual details or patterns on clothes, the sounds or smells in the room, and so on. Then, you would keep associating bodily sensations to all of those details.

As another example, I'll use the fear of driving across a bridge. In your imagination, drive up to the bridge and stop before crossing. Take note of your physical sensations and as many sensory details as possible.

Then, using the FLY ON THE WALL technique (page 68), go where you can watch yourself driving across the bridge. Perhaps you are on a boat in the middle of the river where you can clearly see yourself drive across the bridge. Note the color of the car in front of you. Drive exactly one hundred feet behind it.

For fun, put yourself on a motorcycle. Drive the motorcycle across the bridge as a stunt motorcycle rider. Pull the front wheel off the ground and stand on the seat while riding across the bridge. Take note of your physical sensations and as much sensory detail as possible.

As long as you imagine a scene with many sensory details, and don't let logic prevent you from doing that, your impulsive primitive mind will react and learn. It doesn't even care if you've never ridden a motorcycle and the scene is complete fantasy. If you have a fear of crossing a bridge, it doesn't help to know the odds of having an accident are astronomically low. The fear is based in sensory perception or in the lack of perception caused by a blocking meme. The primitive mind reacts and relates to sensory perception. It's too stupid to know or care if the scene is real or if it's logical. Or perhaps, it is very wise.

TECHNIQUES THAT SUPPORT CATHARTIC TECHNIQUES

The following techniques don't always include cathartic techniques. They help heighten experience by increasing awareness or intensifying sensations. They help you get into the nooks and crannies of your psyche where you can then apply cathartic techniques.

CONNECTED BREATHING

Connected breathing, sometimes known as circular or continuous breathing, is breathing without pausing between your inhale and exhale. It can range from fast and deep to slow and shallow, or from fast and shallow to slow and deep. You can breathe mostly from your diaphragm, or mostly from your chest. However you do it, staying relaxed is essential. One way to make sure of this is to only use as much strength and tension with your inhale that is necessary. Let the exhale fall without controlling it. Don't push when exhaling, and don't hold back on it either. Relaxation is important because the more tense you are, the more likely you will hyperventilate. Hyperventilation doesn't occur if you're relaxed.

Connected breathing is beneficial because it oxygenates your body. It usually relaxes your muscles and nervous system, whether you try to relax or not. It heightens your senses and increases your general awareness of everything. Frequently, we associate tension with heightened awareness, like when taking a test. That can cause an aversion to heightened awareness. With connected breathing, you train yourself to associate high levels of awareness with relaxation and comfort.

How is it useful for catharsis? Connected breathing amplifies your awareness of emotions and bodily sensations. You can get a deeper and more detailed experience of any sensation you want to investigate.

Details and Cautions About Connected Breathing

Rule number one: there are no rules. That is, there's no single right way to do connected breathing. Having said that, here are some suggestions based on what has worked for me. Feel free to disagree and do whatever you feel is best.

First, don't have any expectations. I've used this technique hundreds of times. Most times I haven't experienced any particular emotional charge or drama. Usually I just focus on bodily sensations and tensions as much as I can. They relax and I feel better. However, throughout the rest of the day or even the next day, my typical everyday emotions are usually more accessible and on the surface. Sometimes during a session, old or odd memories pop into my mind. When I do feel strong emotions, I feel them as fully as I can until my body relaxes and the associated anxiety dissipates. Sometimes I have revelations about what the emotions are about, and sometimes I don't. The more I practice, the less interested I am in any thoughts I use to define an emotion or physical sensation.

It's usually a good idea to practice longer than you think you need to. Feeling bored can mean you're done, or it can be a defense mechanism. Knowing the difference takes experience and your best judgment. When I stay with the boredom, it usually transforms into something extremely interesting.

Connected breathing takes some practice. At first, most of your attention will be on maintaining the breathing and trying different types of breathing. I suggest you breathe just a little deeper and faster than normal. When you feel ready, try other ways of breathing, and see how they affect you.

Here's generally what happens with various ways of breathing.

116

- Breathing from the diaphragm, with the stomach rising on the inhale and falling on the exhale: This brings bodily sensations to awareness.
- Breathing from the chest, with the chest expanding on the inhale and deflating on the exhale, and the diaphragm not moving so much: This stimulates the mind and the senses.
- Fast and shallow: This usually makes me feel dreamy but very awake.
- Slow and deep: I often switch to this approach about fifteen minutes into a session. I inhale so slowly that I'm almost to the point of not inhaling. I inhale to the very top of my lungs then let my exhale fall. It is very, very, very relaxing.
- Breathing at a moderate rate: Usually this is when I get the clearest awareness of a particular sense or bodily sensation. With moderate breathing, I can focus more on bodily sensations, and not so much on the mechanics of breathing.
- Fast and deep: I would caution against this technique, especially at the beginning of a session, unless you're sure it's what you want to do. Fast and deep doesn't equal bigger or better. It takes much attention to maintain, so it's harder to be aware of sensations. I only use this when I want to make something as intense as possible, or if I want to be more awake.
- Lying down versus sitting: Now I usually lie down, but when I first started, I would often get sleepy, so I would sit in a chair. Either way it helps if you can stretch, do yoga, get a massage, or something similar before a session to relax muscle tension. Conversely, making muscle tension the subject of your session can also be beneficial.

Relaxation is needed most in the muscles and parts of the body involved with breathing. As your breathing relaxes, your body will follow, but the reverse isn't as true. Relaxed breathing makes less noise then tense breathing. If you can hear your inhale or exhale, you're probably tensing your throat to some degree. Or possibly, you're not in a good position to comfortably open your throat or jaw.

If you're lying down, try putting a pillow under your knees to reduce strain on your lower back. I usually put most of a pillow under my neck so my head tips back a bit. This makes it easier to keep my throat open and relaxed. If you're sitting upright, take note of the muscles you're using to support yourself. See if you can use less muscle tension, or use only the muscles you really need to support yourself.

Focus on each part of your body until it relaxes on its own. You don't need to tell it to relax; attention alone will do the job. Start with your foot, then your shin, knee, thigh, your other foot, shin, knee, thigh, groin, sphincter, diaphragm, lower back, middle back, upper back, shoulder, upper arm, forearm, hand and fingers, your other shoulder, upper arm, forearm, hand and fingers, your neck, jaw (at this point strong relaxation usually occurs), your face (especially around the eyes), forehead, top of head, back of head, around the ears.

How to Deal With Hyperventilation or Paresthesia

When you first practice connected breathing, you might not be completely aware of tension, especially in your inhale or exhale. Tension can cause tingling or numbness in your hands, feet, or lips. This is called paresthesia or tetany. This tingling can be so strong that your hands will take the shape of lobster claws.

Hyperventilation can also cause paresthesia if you're not fully relaxed. Contrary to popular belief, if your body is fully relaxed, you can breathe very fast and deep without hyperventilating.

In either case, paresthesia indicates abnormally low concentration of carbon dioxide in the blood. It's not harmful but it's usually distracting. To dispel tetany or tingling, simply breathe less, slowly or more shallow; or just breathe normally.

MANTRAS

This is strictly my view of what a mantra does, and how I use one. A mantra is a phrase that you repeat for at least twenty minutes. Mantras can be meaningless or meaningful. I prefer a meaningless mantra. I use "Om na ma shi va ya," simply because I learned it many years ago. I'd bet that creating your own mantra would work just as well.

When you repeat a mantra, you replace your usual anxious thoughts with the mantra. The result is that your usual anxiety producing worries go away, at least temporarily. I use a mantra for general relaxation or in place of a nap. It lowers anxiety levels in general and for the rest of the day. I also use a mantra when I have trouble going to sleep.

I'm guessing some people would say I'm using my mantra incorrectly. Maybe so, I've just never been interested in using it for anything else. A web search would give you much free information on how to do it correctly--assuming there really is such a thing as doing it correctly.

I don't see that mantras create catharsis as directly as the cathartic techniques. However, practicing a mantra can induce a relaxed frame of mind that helps with practicing cathartic techniques.

LOOKING AT YOURSELF IN THE MIRROR FOR AN EXTENDED PERIOD OF TIME

This is self explanatory. I've tried this a few times. I can see how it could have a strong emotional charge, but it didn't do much for me. Other people say that it's very interesting and helpful.

Of course, spending an hour grooming in front of the mirror doesn't count. Just look at you, and let that trigger any emotions, thoughts, or bodily sensations. If you like, add the connected breathing techniques already described.

INTERACTION WITH OTHERS USING SEARCH MODE

This exercise will arouse or even create strong bodily sensations you can use to achieve catharsis. It can also develop useful interpersonal and intrapersonal communication skills because you have more comfort with the experience of interacting with others and yourself.

Sit facing another person. You can also do this with a group. Ask yourself, what haven't I noticed about this person before? When you notice something new, tell them so, but don't tell them what it is. Then notice something else you haven't noticed before. The other person will do the same with you simultaneously.

If you agree beforehand, tell the other person what you noticed. This can cause more detailed and dynamic responses but it has the following dangers: it can direct your attention toward your thoughts and decrease attention toward bodily sensations. Saying something that upsets the other person would completely derail the process.

Ask yourself if you are sensing something new about the person with your five senses, or if you are primarily thinking about them and getting new ideas. In time, you might sense qualities about them that don't come from your five senses. You might sense some pain, anger, or a sensitivity you hadn't noticed. In that case, ask a second question. Am I sensing it in them, is that really true of me, or a little of both?

If you know the other person well, your thinking mind tends to dominate and you'll think about past conflicts or fun times together. If you spend twenty minutes or longer doing this, you'll probably become tired of thinking and spend more time sensing them.

I find this technique interesting in terms of how much people focus on each other and themselves. It's also interesting in terms of how much people use their thinking mind, their senses, or their intuition to interact with others. Do you usually talk a lot or do you listen, watch, or sense others? What are the effects of thinking about others or sensing them? Which one do you prefer? Which one do others prefer? Does it matter to you? Do you think it matters to others?

Of course, in terms of catharsis, any answers to those questions aren't as important as asking the questions and benefitting from the search. Catharsis is about comfort with bodily sensations no matter how you usually interact with others. However, the more aware you become of different styles of interaction, the more likely you will try interacting in different ways or in ways that were previously out of your comfort range.

An unexpected effect of this technique, at least for me, is I feel much less annoyed by interactive styles or habits that I don't like. Now I'm more sympathetic toward people who talk nonstop and barely hear the words I manage to get in edgewise. As annoyed as I can get with talkers, I can't help notice that I usually end up with them. I usually listen more than I talk so it mostly works. When I'm with another listener, both of us wait for the other to say something so the conversation doesn't flow so well.

TECHNIQUES USING THOUGHT

The following techniques center on mental processes. They are tools to help you illuminate your thoughts, thought processes, feelings, emotions, and sensations.

GENERALIZATIONS

Unlike a memory that only takes place in the past, a generalized thought can include the past, present, or future. Your general concept of something can include many memories, assumptions about what will happen today, and assumptions about the future.

This technique primarily uses extremes (page 125), to expose the generalizations you have. For example, in general, using the following extremes, what is your opinion of your community?

- My community will always be stable. Everyone will always get along extremely well. All the community services I depend on will always be performed efficiently and for the least cost.
- Conversely, my community will become extremely dangerous. My neighbors will likely rob me. The community officials are corrupt and in cahoots with crime figures. Nothing gets done unless someone gets a bribe.

As another example, my best friend will be my friend for life. We will always have a great time. Conversely, my best friend will soon hate me and never talk to me again.
? How much does _____(person) love me?
? How much do they hate me?

Take note of your bodily sensations while you're imagining either extreme and consider the following:

- Does imagining both extremes make clear the generalization you've been holding?
- Do you feel uncomfortable with your generalization?
- Do you feel doubt about your generalization?

? How can I use the discomfort from my generalization?

I frequently use this technique while walking down the street, or during any activity where I can reflect on the activity. That has the advantage of applying the technique to real things, and people, in my life. Practicing this technique while sitting with eyes closed also has advantages. Here are some general categories you can use for a focused practice, and for using extremes to flush out your generalizations that affect your life.

- you, a simple definition of yourself
- Are you always nice to others or are you more of a bastard than you want to believe?
- your life five years from now
- your mother, father, any member of your family
- a teacher, a friend, an enemy
- coworkers, classmates
- people in general, a group of friends, a community, a country, government
- pain, pleasure
- knowledge
- morality
- your death, existence in general
- God

This exercise is inherently open-minded. If you work with a generalization that is dogmatic or closed-minded, you might feel resistance, discomfort, or anxiety. A belief that is important to you can seem threatened. That doesn't need to be a problem. For example, while practicing this technique, I realized I assumed that when I die, in essence, nothing will change all that much. I will still be me, and I will still be at whatever level I was when I died. I will just take a different form.

As part if this technique, I considered the possibility that when I die that will be it. The light will go out. Nothing of me will exist any longer. My body, and emotions, reacted to that with much discomfort and resistance. So, I put my attention on those sensations. I created comfort with those sensations and the idea of my disintegration into nothingness. However, that didn't really change my belief that I'll take another form when I die. I had to admit, I don't know either way, but I still like to believe that something of me will continue. My belief changed from an assumed belief to a working belief.

Cathartic techniques are generally independent of belief. You can still believe anything you want. If the techniques cause you to change your mind about something, you were probably willing to change your mind before you used the techniques.

Are generalizations good or bad? Should we strive to be free of generalizations? Can we be free of generalizations? Isn't a constant state of doubt a more true way to be? Heck, I dunno. Trying to stop generalizing--generally--seems like too much work. It seems, all we can do is keep and eye on our generalizations, make sure they're working for us and not causing us to make decisions that damage the real things in our lives, such as people.

CONTINUOUS WRITING

Write without stopping for fifteen minutes or longer. This bypasses your ability to censor or lie to yourself. You might find yourself writing the same word or sentence repeatedly, perhaps because you're stuck or because you're cheating. This, of course, would be for you to decide. No one is going to use a red pen to grade what you write.

The primary purpose of this, of course, is to activate and focus on whatever bodily sensations that occur. Apart from that, it can generate ideas you wouldn't generate otherwise. It's good for creativity in writing or just coming up with new solutions to problems. It can be physically stimulating, and mentally exhausting, but in a pleasant way.

A similar process is to talk continuously with another person who is also talking continuously. This also bypasses your ability to censor yourself. While you're talking continuously, you're picking up bits and pieces of what the other person is saying who is also talking continuously. That affects what you say, and that affects what the other person says. It can be an interesting thing to record and listen to later. As a caution, doing this with someone you know can be risky since you're not censoring yourself.

EXTREMES

Using extremes can create a better and more accurate view, both mentally and emotionally, of anything in your life. For the examples below, focus on each of the extremes for at least fifteen minutes, or until you have a catharsis. The subject of these focuses is very broad and deeply ingrained. You might never have a complete or final catharsis with these, but you can certainly gain comfort around them. Note, the first example is mostly thought oriented, but can be emotional as well.

First example: Soon, the world has all the energy it needs via fusion power. Fusion power is clean and relatively safe. The economies of all countries have prospered. World political tensions over energy have faded away. Dictatorships, political repression, and corruption can't survive in such prosperity. There are so many high paying jobs that you only work six months a year. The rest of the time, you pursue your artistic interests. Many other people are living similar lives. Society and culture are more alive than any other time in human history.

The other extreme of this example: The major world economies collapse. War is pervasive everywhere. The people who have the most power and guns in your neighborhood have labeled you an insect, and would kill you on sight. (I could make it much worse and more graphic, but I think you get the idea.)

This next example can be very emotional, but also very beneficial. I consider it an advanced focus. If you feel you're not ready for it to any degree, save it for another time.

Second example: Focus on the nurturing you needed but didn't get. Focus on how your parents or whoever raised you, ignored you, abused you, abandoned you, and so on. Focus on how seldom you were held or hugged. Or maybe you were held and hugged often, but it didn't feel loving. It didn't feel like it had anything to do with you.

The other extreme of this example: Focus on how much affection you received. Focus on how much you were loved and cared for. Maybe your parents didn't show how much they loved you. Maybe they had their own emotional issues to deal with, but if you look, you can find how much they wanted to nurture you and be perfect parents.

MORE DESCRIPTIONS, THEORIES, IDEAS

In this section, I've done my best to describe the techniques and my thinking or theories related to the techniques. However, I couldn't care less if any of the theories are true or false. I should probably explain that brash statement.

In my view, any theory or hypothesis is partly a sales pitch. It's a call for investigation and for proving how accurate the theory is. Is any theory one hundred percent correct? I don't think so. Isn't thinking the sun will rise tomorrow a theory or assumption of truth? It's very very likely the sun will rise tomorrow (although technically it doesn't rise) but anything is possible.

If I keep my left arm straight during my golf swing, I usually get better results. I can think of several reasons or theories for why that is, but does it matter? No, it doesn't matter. I'm just trying to put the ball where I want it to go.

On the other hand, pondering why a mental technique works can give me ideas about other techniques I can try. Those are usually better techniques than if I just randomly try this or that. In that sense, theorizing is worthwhile.

To put it bluntly, if someone said the descriptions in this book are complete bullpucky, I wouldn't disagree with them. However, as of this writing, I fully believe in all the theories or descriptions I've written here. They are currently my best view of the techniques. But hopefully, a year from now, I'll look at any description and feel I have a much better one. We (I) have a need to understand or to associate a mental handle to anything we experience. However, a technique will have an effect whether we have an understanding of it or not.

What you experience when practicing the techniques will create comfort. Without trying the techniques in this book, you will only have yet more ideas that don't really help you feel more comfortable, or help with anything. Practice the techniques but don't take the descriptions and theories of them too seriously. The outcome you get from practicing the techniques is all that matters.

Create your own theories or descriptions of how the techniques work if you want, but don't take those too seriously either. Use theories, descriptions, or mental handles, to the extent they are useful. Be open to and curious about the effect a technique has on you and think of ways to tweak it for even better results.

WHAT IS CATHARSIS?

The Peril of Metaphors

We always use metaphors when discussing or defining mental states and psychological experience. There's not much choice since the mind is so complicated and inaccessible. For example, the words emotion, thought, and awareness, are all metaphors. We don't know exactly what those are or how they work in a concrete sense. We can't touch them or take them apart to see how they work. However, we agree we have those states of mind. For most practical purposes, when we use those words, we are referring to the same thing, even though we can't directly see what we're referring to.

Metaphors can be inaccurate and misleading. Do we repress emotions or do we divert our attention from them? Which is more concrete or accurate? Is saying we have "deep" emotions more accurate than saying we resist some emotions more than others?

If it's clear that your habit of diverting your attention from unwanted experience causes problems, then it's equally clear that focusing your attention on the same experience might be a solution. If it's clear that you stiffen your body when you experience an emotion you don't like, then it's equally clear that letting your body move might help.

If all you know is that you repress your emotions, then what can you do? The word repress isn't concrete or descriptive. It doesn't suggest the exact mental process one might use to repress an emotion, or to fully accept an emotion.

Can you "share" a feeling? If you share an apple, you give part of it away. You have less of your apple. If you express a feeling or emotion, do you have less of anything? You would likely still have the full feeling, plus more awareness of the emotion, plus a connection to another person, plus their feedback.

We talk and think about awareness, emotion, bodily sensations, and catharsis as if we know what these things are. We don't know exactly what they are--but I don't think we need to. It's enough that they are universal experiences, common to us all. We can see that awareness very much affects emotion and bodily sensations--and vice versa. We can play with these elements and see what they can do. We can search for objective truths in how the elements of the psyche interact. We might never find objective truth, but it's worth the effort to try. It's like democracy. We will never achieve a perfect democracy, but we can certainly get closer to that goal if we try.

As an exercise, use the continuous writing technique (page 124) to write down what you feel about something that is bothering you. When you're finished, find any word that describes your emotions or thoughts, and see if you can use a more accurate or more concrete word.

For this book, I've tried to use the most concrete, and more important, the most useful metaphors I can think of. When describing the techniques, I've tried my best to avoid what you might think of as psychobabble or vague language.

With that in mind, I'd like to look at the dictionary definition of catharsis, and dissect its metaphors just a little. I'm primarily looking at definitions three and four. I'm certain the words purging and purifying don't belong in a discussion of psychological catharsis.

ca·thar·sis

n. pl. ca·thar·ses (-sez)

1. Medicine Purgation, especially for the digestive system.
2. A purifying or figurative cleansing of the emotions, especially pity and fear, described by Aristotle as an effect of tragic drama on its audience.
3. A release of emotional tension, as after an overwhelming experience, that restores or refreshes the spirit.
4. Psychology
A technique used to relieve tension and anxiety by bringing repressed feelings and fears to consciousness.
The therapeutic result of this process: abreaction.
Source:
American Psychological Association (APA):
catharsis. (n.d.). The American Heritage® Dictionary of the English Language, Fourth Edition. Retrieved April 11, 2010, from Dictionary.com website: http://dictionary.reference.com/browse/catharsis

Let's look at definition 3. Is anything really "released" during a catharsis? Is that an accurate word for what happens? Is it like releasing a bird from a cage? Is "release" a good metaphor? When a catharsis occurs, I think it's more like you've been traveling down a single lane one-way road (subconscious habitual resistance, diversion of attention, or blocking memes) that suddenly becomes the entire interstate freeway system (assimilation, full integration into the self).

Then there's definition four. To the extent I understand this definition, I don't agree with it. Is bringing repressed feelings and fears to consciousness enough to cause such a result--a catharsis?

The Concrete Elements of Catharsis

Below is a list of metaphors. I consider these essential elements of any catharsis. Physical tension and relaxation might seem to be the most concrete elements in this list, but even they might be metaphorical. Possibly, we only experience a mental representation of any physical sensation and not the sensation itself. For an interesting discussion of the relationship between the body and mind read, The Body Has a Mind of Its Own: How Body Maps in Your Brain Help You Do (Almost) Everything Better, written by Sandra Blakeslee and Matthew Blakeslee.

Despite how metaphorical each element might be, I think the elements are concrete in that everyone understands them. We assume the experience of these elements don't differ very much from one person to another. At least subjectively, we can measure and use these elements. They are as follows:
- resistance, aversion
- anxiety and physical tension
- awareness, attention
- comfort and physical relaxation
- catharsis

Resistance, Aversion

Catharsis resolves resistance and aversion to an experience. Without resistance, there would be no need for catharsis. There could still be physical tension and anxiety, but it would be relatively comfortable, without any aversion. A marathon runner might experience great pain and tension during a long run, yet doesn't feel anxious and doesn't experience that pain as "feeling bad."

Other examples: I feel fear and anxiety when waiting in line for a roller coaster, but I don't resist these feelings. They're part of the fun. When someone parachutes from an airplane, their heart rate could be as high as when they experience strong fear. Because they want to parachute from the plane, they accept and even enjoy the intense physical tension and any fear they might have.

Resisting an experience has similar qualities with our fight, flight, or fright responses. Fighting an experience can include: denial, willfully holding your body still and not

131

responding to an emotion or sensation, defensively tensing your muscles against the experience until it passes. Flight includes diverting your attention to something else or thinking of something else. Fright includes losing consciousness, to any degree, and involuntarily holding your body still.

What causes resistance? Usually (I think), resistance occurs as a reaction to feeling fear or anger, that is, the fight-or-flight response. The stronger either reaction is the less attentive you are to what is happening. You take in less through your senses, evaluate less, and react more. After the initial experience, you're left with a memory that has little conscious detail and an activated nervous system. That memory is usually unpleasant so you resist it.

You can also choose to resist an experience. Let's say you're fourteen years old. One of the popular kids at school says that you frown too much. You want your peers to like and accept you so you train yourself to smile more often. Every time you feel the impulse to frown, you resist it and try to smile instead. After doing that awhile, other kids sense that you're repressing an impulse and comment that your smile seems phony. Until you realize that repressing yourself to please others causes more problems than it solves, you experience much pain and turmoil.

Here's another example of resistance by choice. A marathon runner might spend most of the time during a marathon averting attention from their physical pain. They might think that helps them better endure the marathon. Let's say as an experiment, a fantasy experiment, the neurology department at the local college wants to monitor marathon runners who don't avert their attention from their pain and discomfort while running. The neurology department will pay a runner five thousand dollars if they don't avert their attention. The runner will wear a device that can tell if they avert their attention from their pain. A typical runner would gladly do that for five thousand dollars. They don't normally want to focus attention on their pain and discomfort during a marathon, but they can if they want. In that sense, they don't truly resist the pain and discomfort. They have the ability to feel all the discomfort they have while running, but they choose not to.

For someone who hates running and has a strong resistance to it, it wouldn't matter if they were offered a million dollars. They wouldn't be able to focus their attention on their bodily sensations while running.

Another cause of resistance to your own experiences is simply imitating the resistance patterns of your parents, siblings, or peers. It's debatable exactly how much and how precisely anyone imitates the resistance patterns of anyone else, but I think it's significant.

Deciding when resistance is a problem that you want to resolve, is of course, a matter for your judgment. This book's focus is that resistance is a problem when it includes an inability or reduced ability to focus attention on an experience.

For example, a good friend sneaks up behind you, pokes you in your ribs, and screams at the same time. You jump. Your heart starts racing and your adrenaline level surges. That physical response happens before your conscious mental reaction. When you have a conscious reaction a fraction of a second later, you assume it's someone playing a prank. You turn around and verify your assumption. Even though you were startled, you don't develop a debilitating resistance or blocking meme. Your fright reaction doesn't associate with your friend. There's no reduction in your ability to focus your full attention on your friend. As long as your friend doesn't do that too often, you won't develop resistance.

Conversely, while crossing the street, you suddenly hear a loud horn and screeching tires. Your heart starts racing and your adrenaline level surges. Because the horn and screeching were so loud, you're not sure what just happened. When you turn to look, your nose almost scrapes the grill of a large garbage truck. Several tons of steel almost slammed into your body. A witness verified that you didn't cross the street against the traffic light. The garbage truck was definitely in the wrong but that doesn't help you feel better. You're very confused. You did everything you were supposed to do but you almost died. Now you can't walk anywhere without feeling strong fear and confusion. That fear overwhelms you, and you can't focus enough attention on traffic. You fear you'll have an accident. Unless you can learn how to deal with your fear, your blocking meme, you won't be able to leave your home.

Anxiety and Physical Tension

If there is resistance or aversion to an impulse, or any experience, there is also anxiety and physical tension. Resisting an impulse activates your fight-or-flight response. That activates your sympathetic nervous system (SNS) and causes physical tension. In terms of evolution, your SNS is older than your neocortex and the ideas it produces. It sees your ideas as something external and apart from itself. When your thoughts resist an impulse, your SNS will respond by raising your blood pressure and tense muscles to prepare your body to fight and defend itself. It doesn't know that preparing your body to fight your own thoughts is silly and futile. So, anxiety occurs simply by resisting an impulse or experience.

Your SNS, and the stress it produces, will stay activated for as long as you are able to maintain the idea that an experience should be resisted. If your resistance is strong, you might feel a need to sleep more, or you might feel depressed as a temporary way to rest and relieve the tension.

What is anxiety? For practicing cathartic techniques, it probably doesn't matter. You know when you feel it and when you don't. There is probably no need to define it further. However, I think it's at least interesting so let's define it further anyway.

Anxiety is unwanted stress or an unwanted activation of the sympathetic nervous system. I think it's important to distinguish between wanted and unwanted stress. Unwanted stress has much different effects than wanted stress. Unwanted stress can cause ill health, neurosis or psychological trauma. Wanted stress can be exciting and life affirming. I want to feel the stress and fear I feel when riding a roller coaster, so I wouldn't say I feel anxiety. My preference is to only define anxiety as unwanted stress. Wanted stress is excitement, arousal, stimulation or just fun.

So then, what causes you to resist some types of stress, and want other types? To complicate it even more, what causes you to enjoy something one day, and at another time, the same experience hurts? For example, a friend who teases you can be fun and playful. On anther day you feel hurt.

Is there any particular experience that anyone would always resist? So far, I can't think of one. For any experience you would normally resist, there is a possible situation where you would willfully submit to the same experience. A martyr accepts whatever stress they experience, at least enough to get through committing suicide. No one would want to experience a bear attacking them. But what if you're testing a suit that was specifically designed to resist a bear attack? Troy Hurtubise at least attempted that test.

Maybe no particular experience always causes anxiety but overwhelm will usually cause anxiety. Feeling shy or defensive toward others will stimulate your SNS but you won't feel anxiety until you've felt it too much or for too long. Drinking too much coffee will cause stress. When you've felt that stress longer than you can stand, that stress becomes anxiety. Any task that overwhelms your ability to complete it can cause anxiety.

A task that seems overwhelming will cause anxiety until you remind yourself that you can only do what you can do, step by step, or until you fully accept that you might fail. Overstimulation of your body (too much coffee, bad food, and so on) is easy enough to remedy. Any cognitive habit like feeling shy or defensive, and the stress it causes, can also be resolved (see CONNECTONS AND ASSOCIATIONS , page 47).

Awareness, Attention

Attention or awareness is the road to catharsis. A resisted memory gets almost no attention. As soon as you're aware of the memory, you divert your attention away from it. This diversion can become habitual and subconscious. Even if the memory is completely forgotten on a conscious level, the physical tension never goes away.

Diverting your attention away from something that's trying to enter your awareness is more work. Don't think of a pink elephant! But you just did, didn't you? To not think of a pink elephant, first you must think of one, and then add one or more steps to divert your attention.

The physical tension of a repressed experience never subsides, but the associated memory can be forgotten. So, applying attention to bodily tension is the key to breaking the habit of diversion, and to relaxing the tension. Intentionally and willfully focusing attention on bodily sensations, inherently and immediately, reverses diversion or repression.

Comfort and Physical Relaxation

Relaxation starts almost immediately after starting to focus on bodily sensations. A significant relaxation usually occurs after ten or fifteen minutes. Why does this happen? I don't know. It just does.

As an experiment, focus on your jaw muscles for at least twenty minutes, without trying to relax your jaw. Simply keep bringing your attention back to your jaw every time you notice your mind has wandered. What you're likely to notice is that your jaw spontaneously relaxes on its own. If you're curious about this phenomenon, a good book to read is The Relaxation Response, by Dr. Herbert Benson.

To be clear, catharsis doesn't always get rid of tension associated with an experience or memory. If the subject of a catharsis is inherently tense, only the resistance is relieved. Someone who has a catharsis about riding roller coasters will have tension and stress while waiting in line for the roller coaster just like everyone else. However, they'll no longer have resistance, or feel anxiety about that stress. The stress is part of the fun.

Catharsis

Once your other faculties see that you're serious about staying with a focus on your bodily sensations, they will join in the effort. Your thoughts, memories or any other experience, consciously or subconsciously, will start associating with the sensations that you've stopped resisting.

Your faculties will start talking to each other: "I guess we're not resisting this anymore. What's this sensation about? I don't know. Why am I thinking about that dog that attacked? That feels right. Let's go with that. Anyone know why that dog bit? As I recall the dog was lying on its side ... hey, it had babies, that's right! I think that's it!"

Your mind, consciously or subconsciously, will start processing and thinking about the bodily sensations you bring to awareness. Your mind will try to define the sensations or associate a mental handle. It will free associate and find an idea that fits the sensations. Working in this manner, your mind will connect the sensations to other thoughts, emotions, memories, and experiences.

At some point, when you've spent enough time associating, free associating, and connecting to other experiences, you will have a catharsis and a perceptual shift. Your sensations and any associated thoughts will assimilate into your sense of self. When you have spent enough time associating, the resisted experience will suddenly cross over to being fully accepted. Either the fight-or-flight response will no longer be a part of the experience, or it will take on a playful nature, like when you pretend to fight someone or run away. When resistance crosses over to full acceptance, you'll not only feel a strong physical relaxation, but an existential relaxation as well. By existential, I mean you'll feel better about existing. You have reclaimed part of yourself. Life seems like a better deal than before.

After a catharsis, because the pain of resistance is gone, usually there is no need to ponder further, or create rationalizations about the experience. Unless the new associations are useful for a current goal, they will fade away from lack of use.

What Catharsis Does and Doesn't Do

Catharsis will relieve pain and fear caused by resisting your own experience, that is, neurotic pain or neurotic fear. Catharsis doesn't relieve real pain and real fear.

By focusing on physical sensations, neurotic pain will simply go away. When you're ready, and can fully focus on all aspects of a particular neurotic resisted pain, it will naturally resolve itself. Your subconscious will bring to your awareness what you're most ready to focus on. Trying to force a resolution of a particular pain or fear can cause new anxiety and stress.

Real pain or fear won't go away until there is a real resolution. If there is a real threat near you or in your thoughts, your autonomic nervous system will, and should, react. For example, if you walk by an angry growling dog, you'll likely be afraid. If you need to walk by that same angry dog every day on your way to work, just thinking about it could arouse fear. There's nothing to be afraid of from your thoughts about the dog, but the thoughts are about a real unresolved ongoing issue.

Of course, the tendency to resist fear and pain is strong. But for this example, let's assume you don't at all resist the fear you have about the dog. Because you're not resisting, you're more able to think of solutions. You could talk to the owner and hope they will sympathize with you, file a police report, or spray the dog with repellent. Even before you try any of those, you'll feel some relief in that those possibilities give you hope. So, catharsis doesn't directly resolve real pain or fear, but it makes you more able to resolve them. It enables you to bring your full attention to any issue.

How do you tell the difference between neurotic pain and real pain? I think most of us would agree that pain based on resisting your own experience is not real pain. Most of us would agree that fear caused by imminent physical danger is definitely real fear and could become real physical pain if the threat isn't resolved.

Everything between those extremes is debatable and very subjective. For example, is the fear of public speaking a real fear? It's frequently stated the fear of public speaking is stronger than the fear of death for many people. What's the worst that could happen if you give a bad speech? Everyone who heard your speech might shun you. Possibly, you could lose your job. Is that worse than death? Let's say the fear of public speaking is so strong due to genetic memory (see page 74), and we are born with this fear. When we lived in tribes, being shunned by the tribe could easily be life threatening. Is a fear that you're born with a real fear? Maybe it's more real than a fear of crossing a bridge, but less real than someone pointing a gun at you.

Let's say the angry dog that you had to walk by daily, died. Your autonomic nervous system still reacts with fear every time you walk by the house where the dog lived. Is that fear less real than when the dog was alive?

For catharsis, these questions aren't important. There's no need to decide how real pain or fear is. That can create even more resistance, frustration and repression.

Catharsis occurs when all of your faculties have sufficiently processed an experience. The thinking mind is only one part of your mind. It doesn't have access to all parts of you and it can't control or meaningfully affect all parts of you. The thinking conscious mind can't know when sensations, thoughts, and emotions will assimilate. It can't know what you most need to assimilate. However, it will likely try to ponder what real pain is, and what it isn't. It is a fascinating question but it's mostly academic. It generally doesn't help with catharsis.

So, the trick is letting your pain and fear find their way. There's no need to decide whether pain is real or not. If you have pain or fear that you think should have assimilated by now, you're wrong. Let your mind, and bodily sensations, work on resolutions for any pain or fear, but don't be surprised if you don't find any resolutions. Sometimes, catharsis is realizing you might have a particular fear or pain for the rest of your life. Then, three days later, assimilation overwhelms you while you're making toast.

WHAT IS THE PROBLEM THAT CATHARSIS SOLVES?

The problem is resistance to your own experience. In general, feeling bad, or feeling anxiety includes some amount of resistance or aversion toward your experience. Frequently, resistance to pain is much more painful than actual pain.

Let's get back to our marathon runners. Running a twenty-six mile marathon can be very painful, but seasoned marathoners have little resistance to this pain. They see it as part of something they want to do. If you asked them if running a marathon is too painful, they'd shrug their shoulders and say no, not really, or I guess so. A marathoner can experience a great deal of pain, yet not experience it as "feeling bad." Other people might run only as far as a city block, feel great resistance to their pain, and then refuse to continue. You wouldn't have to ask them if they felt too much pain; they would tell you anyway.

If you resist something every time you sense it, that resistance becomes an ingrained habit, a meme. You habitually divert your attention from whatever you don't want to experience. After a while, you aren't aware you're resisting anything, but stress or anxiety from the experience is still in your reactions and in your body. By diverting your attention from the experience, you lose the opportunity to view the experience in a different way and you lose access to any information in the experience.

Daily living can reinforce a habit of resistance and diverting attention. For example, if you have resistance to how you react to people or to how they treat you, you'll have daily discomfort. If you usually feel shy or inferior to everyone else, it can be a nearly constant torture. If you usually feel people will take advantage of you when you let your guard down, constantly being on guard can drain your energy. Our minds associate anything we're experiencing with anything we've experienced before that is similar. So, if you're uncomfortably shy, there will be plenty of people around to remind you of that, and to reinforce your resistance to feeling that way. The habit of diverting your attention from the unwanted experience (usually called repression) just gets stronger.

Habitual resistance preoccupies our minds, robs our energy, and can be very painful. We think that resisting something will make it go away, yet our subconscious mind keeps bringing it up again and again. We obsess about fears that will probably never come about: Will I lose my job? Do people respect me? Is my spouse interested in someone else? Does anyone love me? Did I turn off the stove? We can have anxiety over things that don't exist. We can have anxieties that don't help us in any way.

It gets worse. When you habitually divert attention from something you sense, either you literally forget it exists, or you pretend it's not important. You dissociate from all aspects of the experience--the physical sensations, associated thoughts, and emotions. You don't see it as part of yourself even though it is. You create reasons and rationalizations for why you feel anxiety that have nothing to do with the anxiety. It's like convincing yourself that you

141

don't have a coffee table in the middle of your living room, and then making up neurotic delusional reasons for why your shins have bruises.

Eventually, it doesn't even matter what originally caused you to resist and divert awareness from an experience. You've developed a habit that has a life of its own. Even if you accurately remember the original reason for resisting an experience, that doesn't necessarily break the habit of feeling stress, fighting yourself, and diverting your attention from the experience.

Any catharsis will break the habit of diverting attention from a resisted experience. When you no longer resist an experience, comfort quickly follows. You see the experience as part of yourself and as part of all acceptable experience. Your general anxiety lessens. Less anxiety makes life seem better. You might have spent years building and developing a particular habit of resistance, but you can resolve it in minutes. Once an experience is fully comfortable, the habit of diverting attention from that experience doesn't return.

When you're anxious and fear you will lose your job, you're not anxious about losing your job; you're anxious because you don't want to feel the sensations associated with that fear. If you have no resistance to the bodily sensations, then the possibility of losing your job becomes a simple matter of fact: either it will happen, or it won't. The outcome becomes almost academic. It might indeed be possible to lose your job, but you can still do your best.

Possibly the fear entered your mind in the first place because you subconsciously sensed that your boss has a low opinion of your work. If there is no resistance to the idea of losing your job, you're more likely to consider taking action that can help you keep your job. The scenario could be something like: I'm worried about losing my job - am I messing up somehow - did I forget something - oh, that's right, my boss wanted me to finish that project - I better do that.

If there is resistance, on the other hand, the scenario could be something more like this: You're worried about losing your job - you resist that idea and the associated sensations - confusion and stress - you don't know what to do - the feeling won't go away so you try to ignore it by thinking of something else. This second scenario will just keep repeating and repeating, and it won't help with anything.

WITH CATHARSIS, ANXIETY IS COMPLETELY RESOLVED

As soon as you resist an impulse, your sympathetic nervous system (SNS) activates to some degree. Your SNS sees the resistance as fighting the impulse. The SNS prepares your body to react with the fight-or-flight response. By its nature, the SNS doesn't include pondering, reflection, or awareness in general. It includes one basic decision: fight or run away. If you repeatedly resist an impulse, you create an ingrained habitual response that includes tension that comes with activating your SNS. Mentally, since you don't recognize that you're resisting the impulse, it's easy to create delusional reasons or excuses for why you habitually feel tense, such as, I'm weak and can't control my animal nature, and so on.

Once catharsis is achieved, an impulse becomes a simple option or a memory. There is no longer resistance to experiencing the impulse so the sympathetic nervous system doesn't activate. The fight-or-flight response is no longer part of the impulse. You no longer need to find excuses for experiencing the impulse. Even though you might have resisted an impulse for many years, the resistance and the fight-or-flight response never return. The impulse doesn't go away but the resistance to it and the fight-or-flight response completely and immediately dissolves. You experience the impulse as part of yourself, and as something that you fully and comfortably accept.

For example, Sara was very afraid of mice. If she saw a mouse, she would run to the opposite corner of the room. If there was a chair or table available, she would jump onto it.

Until she was sure the mouse was gone, she would yell and plead for someone to get the mouse.

While on a picnic, Sara's friend was frightened by a mouse that she saw in a garbage can. Sara was very curious. She instinctively or subconsciously knew that she could look at the mouse in the garbage can. She knew the mouse couldn't jump out and hurt her. She watched the mouse for a few minutes. She noticed how fast its heart was beating and how frightened it looked. Then Sara turned the garbage can on its side and watched the mouse run away into some tall grass. After that experience, Sara was no longer afraid of mice.

Sara's catharsis came about by happenstance, instead of deliberately using cathartic techniques, but it is still a good example of catharsis. She spent time being aware of the mouse by watching it. She was aware in detail by noticing the mouse seemed frightened. She was curious (search mode). That single experience was all she needed to assimilate her experience of mice in general. She realized the worst that could happen in her home is that a mouse would run over her toes while desperately trying to get away from her.

CATHARSIS ONLY ENGAGES IMPULSES

Achieving catharsis does not include an effort to reduce or alter an impulse in any way. With catharsis, an impulse might recur as often as ever but since there's no resistance, you can indulge it or not. If you repeatedly choose not to focus on it, you'll barely notice the impulse as time passes. It won't come into your conscious awareness.

Cathartic techniques don't include conditioning, retraining, or reeducating an impulse. Trying to retrain an impulse inherently, to some degree, resists the impulse since there's an attempt to change the impulse.

144

Let's say Jack tries to retrain his shyness about Anabel, instead of using cathartic techniques to unite his sensations with his thoughts. Whenever he feels fear or shyness about asking Anabel for a date, he counters that with positive affirmations like: I have options and can react comfortably if she rejects me. I'm likeable. For all I know, Anabel wants me to ask her for a date.

Those affirmations help Jack to feel more confident. They are helpful thoughts, but the physical reaction from his fear is still fully active and unchanged. Jack's goal is to replace or retrain his feelings of fear with the feelings the affirmations provide. However, those affirmations don't add any direct awareness to the physical sensations or the general experience of feeling shy and afraid. The affirmations only mentally counter the sensations of his fear. Jack can experience the confidence the affirmations provide, but only if he keeps repeating the affirmations. If he keeps repeating the affirmations, he will develop a habit, and habitually feel the benefits of the affirmations. However, the habit will still include the tension from his unassimilated fear and activated ANS (autonomic nervous system).

Jack's affirmations might be more than enough to help him talk to Anabel and to ask her out for a date, but he still feels uncomfortable. The interactions between him and Anabel don't flow easily. To some degree, Jack is tense the entire time he's with Anabel even though all appears to be going well.

Conversely, if Jack focuses attention on his sensations of fear and shyness, the sensations become relaxed and comfortable. Since the sensations are in Jack's awareness directly and for relatively long periods, his thinking mind accepts the sensations and ponders them. Jack naturally starts considering aspects of his shyness and aspects of Anabel that he hadn't before. He doesn't need to spend time and effort trying to counter his fear. He doesn't need to retrain his impulses. He only becomes more aware of his current sensations. Possibly, his fear impulse with Anabel won't change except that Jack no longer resists it, and his

ANS doesn't activate and cause tension. He will likely make jokes about it or just tell Anabel he feels it for whatever reason.

Possibly, Anabel will think Jack is crazy. More likely, she will appreciate that Jack can describe what he feels. She might even tell him that many people are shy with her and she's not sure why. It's something she would like to investigate. Intimacy and a strong connection could develop between Jack and Anabel. Intimacy is less likely to occur if Jack avoids awareness of his fear or shyness by countering them with affirmations.

WHAT YOU CAN EXPECT WHEN PRACTICING THE TECHNIQUES OF CORE CATHARSIS?

Ideally, don't expect anything. Feeling surprised is an indication that you're doing the techniques correctly--to the extent there is such a thing as doing them correctly. Feeling surprised is an indication that you're paying attention and being open. Having said that, here are some general descriptions of what it can be like when directly focusing on bodily sensations longer than you ever have before.

When practicing a focused session (sitting with eyes closed), it usually takes about five minutes to settle into the process. At first, your thinking mind will chatter away and distract you from focusing on bodily sensations. After that, you'll have more success holding a focus on sensations, and for longer periods. With practice, you'll get better at seeing the difference between distracting random thoughts, and thoughts that come from a sensation. Whenever you can, try to associate or connect random thoughts to your sensations. That way, you'll no longer experience them as distracting.

After about fifteen minutes, you'll usually feel some relaxation. You might get sleepy. Sleepiness normally causes some unconsciousness. With practice, you'll be able to focus clearly while your body relaxes. You won't get sleepy.

Some people believe that sleepiness can be a way to avoid a particular experience. I'm not sure if that has been true for me. After focusing on the sensations of sleepiness, I have less trouble falling asleep at night. Now I can recognize and indulge these sensations more easily.

After fifteen minutes or so, you might start feeling bored and wonder why you were tense in the first place. A catharsis can be mild, or its sense of relief can wash over you like a tidal wave--or anything between those extremes. Don't mistake relaxation for catharsis. Catharsis is full assimilation. It's the point when you know you'll never resist a particular sensation again. However, relaxation and a sense of release usually happen with full assimilation. With experience, the difference becomes clearer between only relaxation, versus the relaxation that accompanies assimilation.

Once you've relaxed, you might feel like nothing is happening. It gets more difficult to feel sensations. You might think you're not feeling anything, but that's never true. You're always feeling something, even if the sensations are very subtle. In fact, subtle sensations can be especially interesting, especially sensations that you have never brought to awareness before. You can bring subtle anxieties to mind that you've had all of your life and have never consciously experienced before.

Any of the techniques in this book might only direct your attention to bodily sensations for a fraction of a second. The reactive thinking mind can be strong. You'll feel a sensation, and then get lost in the interpretation of that sensation or a random fantasy. You'll realize you're doing this and use a technique to direct your attention back to your sensations. Frequently, the process involves repeatedly bringing your attention back to bodily sensations, if only for another fraction of a second.

We don't usually spend much time focusing on and being aware of sensations. Usually, as soon as we sense something in our body, we immediately define what the sensation is and stop focusing on the sensation. We think about what the sensation is like, or other mental associations come to mind. The sensation reminds us of something and we start thinking about that. The cathartic approach involves focusing on bodily sensations for much longer than you ever have.

With my first sessions, when I realized that I was indulging a thought or emotion, I felt like a failure. Now if I get an interesting revelation or emotion, I'll indulge it for a few minutes. I'd rather do that then feel pressured. And the more I practice these techniques, the more I realize there's plenty of time. Experimenting and playing is okay. If you spend thirty minutes trying to focus on bodily sensations, and only hold your attention on your sensations a total of three seconds, you've done fine. Three seconds is likely many times longer than you've ever directly focused on those sensations before. If nothing else, thirty minutes of sitting still is always good.

The more you focus on sensations, the more they'll associate with and interact with other sensations, thoughts, and emotions. The more this association occurs, the closer you get to catharsis.

Cathartic processing can be most difficult with your first few attempts. It can be scary. With a little practice, however, you'll soon see that any emotion that comes up isn't really a problem. You'll discover that intentionally focusing on an experience in more detail, immediately starts assimilation and relief from resistance. With some success, you'll see that it's really an easy process.

At first, you might not be able to make a clear distinction between bodily sensations and emotion, but this gets easier with practice. At first, you might go for several minutes before you remember what you're doing. It's easy to become distracted by a thought, an emotion, or to get sleepy. There's no need to get mad or scold yourself if you lose concentration. If you do get mad at yourself, you can always focus on the sensations associated with that. All sessions are at least a little different. Look for how they are different. The same sensation will be a little different from one second to the next. Expecting anything in particular to happen is a thought, and not a focus on bodily sensations. The primary goal is not to achieve a catharsis. Trying to achieve a catharsis is counterproductive. The primary goal is focusing attention on bodily sensations. Catharsis spontaneously comes from that focus.

This is a very general description of what practicing the techniques is like. There are many exceptions. Please keep in mind that you could experience something completely different than I've just described, and the process can be very different each time you do it. Describing the process at all is misleading to some degree, but I've decided it might be helpful, so I've included it.

Can You Use Cathartic Techniques to Cure All of Your Anxiety? Probably, But Why Would You Want To?

Personally, I like anxiety, fear, and pain to some degree. They all make me feel alive. I feel I'm fully living if I find my limits. If I don't feel exhausted to some degree at the end of the day, I don't feel like I've tried. In some ways, I feel more pain and anxiety then ever. I try harder. I exhaust myself more often simply because I know I can fully relax anytime I feel the need. I have no fear that anxiety will overwhelm me for too long. If I feel resistance, I can always process it.

That's why in my personal examples, I mention that I still feel depressed and anxious at times. But I like feeling those. It means I'm fully living. So, yes, I suppose the cathartic techniques could cure all of your anxiety, but that's not something I've wanted to do.

Hypnagogic or Hypnic Jerk

Most people have experienced a bodily twitch just as they fall asleep. This is called a hypnagogic or hypnic jerk. Why this happens isn't really understood, but it's common and considered normal. If you've never experienced a hypnic jerk, it feels as if you're falling and your mind jerks you awake to prevent it. At least, that's the most popular explanation. For me, hypnic jerks happen when I haven't planned to go to sleep just yet, but I fall asleep anyway. I twitch and shake myself awake, feeling angry that I went to sleep. Then I usually change my mind (turn off the TV) and decide that now would be a good time to go to sleep.

Hypnic jerks can also occur while focusing on bodily sensations. I assume this happens for a similar reason. When you have a sudden and strong relaxation, or when you get sleepy, your mind isn't sure what's happening and it shakes your body to you wake you.

WHY DO WE FIGHT OUR OWN EXPERIENCE?

I certainly don't know for sure (and I don't think anyone does), but this viewpoint might be helpful. The short answer is--because we can. We can be aware of our primitive mind's impulses (see, THE REPTILIAN AND MAMMALIAN MINDS, page 162) and wish they didn't happen. Our higher thinking mind can easily forget that our reptilian mind is part of the same brain and same self. The conscious thinking mind can be arrogant. When our thinking mind doesn't understand an impulse, we conclude it shouldn't happen. We decide that a craving is pointless and should never occur. Our higher thinking brain tries to reject the unwanted impulses that our lower primitive brain produces.

However, our thinking mind can only resist an impulse by-- thinking. We can rationalize this or that. We can pretend our impulses don't exist or don't matter, but our impulses definitely exist. Our ingrained autonomic habits have a mind of their own and will happen dispite what we think about them or any rationale we use to explain them. In the fight between the thinking mind and an impulse, an impulse has a huge advantage. It's ingrained, automatic, and will stay active as long as we stay alive.

Take any impulse and decide that it will never bother you again. With your conscious thinking mind, command that an impulse never return. Would that work? Does your thinking mind have that power? If it did, everyone would already be completely happy just by telling our unwanted feelings and thoughts to never return.

When our thinking mind resists an impulse, that fight activates our sympathetic nervous system so we can better defend ourselves (see, THE AUTONOMIC NERVOUS SYSTEM, page 161). That's just what the sympathetic nervous system does. That's its job. It works very well when truly needed. It has likely saved your life many times. The problem is, fighting an impulse is fighting you and there is no winning. All we get from that is anxiety. I wonder if any other mammal can fight their own experience. Or are we humans the only mammal with that affliction due to our large and complex neocortex?

Additionally, our fight, flight, or fright responses usually make us unconscious. We lose the ability to consciously evaluate what is happening in detail. The stronger the fight, flight, or fright responses, the more we act from instinct and the less aware we are.

After a frightening incident, we have a memory that is mostly unconscious and a response that is involuntary. All of that can take place within our primitive brain. When we remember the frightening incident, we remember our reaction and little else. Details of the incident won't come to awareness unless we try to bring them to awareness. Afterward, we're at least aware of our uncomfortable response, and we usually resist the memory of the incident.

Let's say when you were four years old a dog growled at you and tried to bite you. After that incident, you subconsciously generalized that all dogs are frightening. Whenever you saw any dog, you automatically became frightened. Other kids teased you because you were afraid of harmless dogs. You couldn't help it and just cried. You hated your response but it was automatic; you could do nothing about it. Then your brother, who was present when the dog tried to bite you, tells you the dog snapped at you because you pulled its tail. Now you start remembering all the details of when that dog tried to bite you. Now you have much more of a memory than just the fright response. At four years old, you can reason that if you don't pull a dog's tail, you can probably pet it. After cautiously petting a few dogs, your ingrained fright response melts away. While petting those dogs, you still felt your fright response, but you didn't resist the feelings or withdraw awareness from the feelings. Because you focused awareness on the feelings, the feelings relaxed.

USING BODILY SENSATIONS AS THE PRIMARY FOCUS

First, here's an old joke. A man leaves a restaurant and sees a friend of his searching the ground under a streetlight. His friend says he dropped his car keys and asked if the man would help search for them. They find some coins and an earring but no car keys. The man asks, "Are you sure you dropped your keys here?" His friend says, "No, actually, I think I dropped them when I got out of my car." Irritated, the man asks, "Then why are you looking here?" His friend says, "Because the light's better here."

Do we use our thinking mind to deal with feelings simply because it's always there and never shuts up? Even when we experience emotions and bodily sensations directly, our thinking mind needs to interpret and define them. How much do those definitions help us to feel more comfortable compared to resolving resistance, and simply directing attention toward sensations, emotions, and feelings?

I don't think there's a definite answer to those questions. Of course, the viewpoint of this book is the thinking mind is not the best tool for dealing with emotions and anxiety. At best, our interpretations and definitions of our feelings help but not nearly as much as: resolving resistance, resolving the inability to be aware of sensations, resolving the habit of diverting attention from bodily sensations.

At worse, our thinking mind creates delusion and causes us to move further and further away from the direct experience of our bodily sensations and emotions.

Some Reasons for Using Bodily Sensations As the Primary Focus

- Because bodily sensations are a more direct and efficient route toward comfort. You feel comfort or discomfort in and from your body. Your thinking mind doesn't feel anything. It's a machine. If you didn't have a body, or you were completely numb, all of your experience would be mental and academic. You wouldn't have anxiety, fear, anger or cravings. The thinking mind doesn't directly cause physical stress or anxiety. Fear, and the stress it creates, can happen whether you think about it or not. You don't need to think to feel overwhelmed or feel the stress it creates. You can even ponder conflicting thoughts without issue until you decide, consciously or not, to resist one or both thoughts. You decide one or the other must be false since both can't be true.
- When you focus on bodily sensations, they naturally become more comfortable. Any resistance to the sensations naturally dissipates. If you instruct your mind to associate comfortable meanings and ideas with your bodily comfort, your mind will creatively comply. The reverse is not always true. If you use the affirmation, "My body now feels better than it ever has before.", does your body suddenly feel better than it ever has before? Positive thinking doesn't directly affect ingrained patterns of bodily stress and

153

anxiety. A mental understanding of your motivations or emotions can also have little effect on bodily stress and anxiety. However, positive thinking and understanding bring comfort to the extent that either directs attention toward your bodily sensations.

Why use bodily sensations as the primary focus? Because that's where we lost our keys. Just because the thinking mind is so active and dominant, doesn't mean it's the best tool for feeling more comfortable.

Here's an example that might help illustrate the point. Imagine sitting in a comfortable chair in your home. For the next thirty minutes, you will think about something that you feel anxious about. You will think about it in every way you can. You will think about how to best resolve your anxiety.

Compare that to a slightly different scenario. For the next thirty minutes, you will think about something that you feel anxious about. However, this time, you will spend the thirty minutes in a soothing hot tub. No matter what you think about, your ideas will associate with much more physical comfort than doing the same process while sitting in a chair. Your thinking mind will easily create positive rational ideas. What you previously felt anxious about will feel comfortable, simply because the warm water soothed your bodily sensations while you imagined what previously made you anxious.

I'm not suggesting you find a hot tub for practicing the techniques. When practicing cathartic techniques, physical comfort comes from directing attention toward sensations, the relaxation response, and reversal of resistance. These elements more thoroughly affect catharsis than only sitting in a hot tub. However, practicing the techniques while sitting in a hot tub could be interesting.

As another example, let's say you need to speak in front of large groups for your job but you get so anxious that you just can't do it. A supportive coworker tells you there is really nothing to worry about, and if you just memorize your main points, you can do it. That idea makes sense to you. You have a new understanding or viewpoint that helps. Because of that understanding, you tell yourself the fear is not real. As long as you present your speaking points clearly, the audience will enjoy your speech even if you make a mistake or two. In fact, you've realized that people like it if you make an occasional mistake.

That new viewpoint makes you comfortable enough to speak in front of a large group. BUT, you still feel physical tension and fear before every speech you make. You still feel uncomfortable physical tension, fear, and anxiety. Your body hasn't come to the same realization as your mind. You need a catharsis that includes your body.

Over time, you would probably be more and more physically comfortable, even if you were only working from a new mental viewpoint. Every time you give a speech, you would experience the associated bodily sensation and anxiety if only for spit second. It seems as if those split seconds eventually add up, and the sensations also become comfortable. The sensations associate and connect to enough of you that you don't experience them as uncomfortable sensations. I guess the question is, do you want to wait that long?

DIFFICULTY FACING RESISTED EXPERIENCE

You might ask, isn't it best to repress an experience that you spontaneously resist? Maybe a memory can be too painful to remember and relive. Why isn't repression a valid option?

There are no definitive answers to these questions. Possibly, even though repression and its anxiety cause disease and strife, your karmic destiny requires it. Maybe you shouldn't be happy--this lifetime. This is a matter of philosophy and faith. Since you've read this far, you probably have faith that life can be free of pointless anxiety. The techniques of this book are based on that faith.

Don't we face painful repressed experience, sooner or later, no matter what we do? And don't we feel great because of it? Isn't a good cry, finally, facing sensations you've been repressing?

I want to reiterate, with these techniques, you'll likely spend much longer periods focusing on painful resisted or repressed experience than you've probably ever imagined. When I describe this process, some people have trouble understanding what I'm saying even though I repeat it several times. Many people, when they do hear it, and understand it, look at me as if I'm crazy. They think that if they intentionally focus on something they've been repressing, their anxiety will keep increasing until it's overwhelming. I've found, over and over, that any anxiety I feel is rarely too much to engage fully. The physical stress that anxiety puts on your body is usually much less than running around the block. It's not difficult to feel it for twenty minutes, or several hours if needed. I assume you've felt very anxious about something for several hours or even weeks. You just didn't do it on purpose, for a purpose, and with acceptance. Adding those elements creates a completely different experience.

As concretely as I can, here are several points on why the cathartic process is easy. Because you look for more detail in a sensation, you're no longer resisting the sensation. Because you're no longer resisting the sensation, unnecessary muscle tension or nervous system tension starts to relax. You immediately start to feel relief.

Resistance to an experience is really the source of pain. Anticipation of pain is frequently more painful than the pain itself. Telling a child they will be spanked in ten minutes is much more cruel than spanking the child immediately. The fear of fear can induce a panic attack, even when the anticipated fear never occurs and isn't likely to occur.

Frequently, we sense a bodily sensation and respond to it with a thought or emotion, or both. Then we stop focusing on the sensation. If we investigate any part of that process, we think about the logic of the thoughts or we try to define or analyze an emotion. We don't usually look for more detail in the bodily sensation. The cathartic techniques are the opposite of that.

Because the primary focus is on sensation, any associated thoughts or emotions don't get so much attention. Your thinking mind becomes a partner to what your bodily sensations need and not vice versa. There's no magic. You're mind will gladly comply and help focus on sensations especially after you have some success with the techniques. Your mind will create comfortable ideas that correspond to your physical comfort.

In a sense, you're diverting your attention from your thoughts and emotions as soon as you have them. In a sense, you're "repressing" your thoughts and emotions so you don't experience much pain from them. However, each time you find more detail about a bodily sensation, you also find more detail with associated thoughts and emotions, since they also come back into awareness. Over time, you process your thoughts and emotions more extensively than ever, even though you're not trying to do that.

You've probably experienced that many times when you've had a good cry. During a good cry, your primary focus of attention naturally goes toward your bodily sensations. From the strong emotions you experience during the cry, you tend to think about and review the situation you're crying about. After a while, your body starts to relax and you feel better physically. You have more mental clarity about what was distressing you and it doesn't seem as bad as before. Crying is a natural and spontaneous cathartic process. By intentionally focusing on bodily sensations, we can apply that same cathartic process to anything we want without waiting for it to be so painful that we feel compelled to cry.

157

By making thoughts and emotions secondary, does that mean they don't matter? Yes and no. The goal is to focus on a sensation long enough that it fully assimilates and catharsis occurs. In that sense, any thoughts and emotions that occur during a focus are just by-products of the focus on a bodily sensation. On the other hand, very profound, enlightening, and useful thoughts can occur while focusing on sensations. Your thoughts were informed or counseled by your sensations. How useful your thoughts seem, is of course, up to your best judgment.

Your thinking mind needs reason and meaning. If you let it, it will find all the meaning it needs to make sense of your newfound physical comfort. It will follow the inherent wisdom in your bodily sensations. Your mind can do that with ease since it is immensely creative. Consider all the wild dreams your mind has created.

When focusing on bodily sensations, you might experience a memory far more than you ever have before. However, don't assume that reliving a memory, directly or indirectly, is important for anxiety relief or general comfort. Sometimes, it can be a distraction. Catharsis can also occur from focusing only on physical sensations and without experiencing any associated thoughts, memories or emotions. Associated thoughts or memories might have been completely forgotten, or the bodily sensation never had any associated thoughts or emotions.

Another way the techniques are easy is that you pick the subject of the focus. Generally speaking, you won't pick something that is too painful. If you do, you'll stop focusing on it. You'll go back to repressing it. In that case, you should repress it, at least for now.

For me, pain isn't the primary factor in what I decide to engage. Sometimes, I'll very much want to focus on something that is very painful as soon as it occurs to me. Other times, I'll pass on something that is barely painful. My gut tells me I'm not ready or I don't need to focus on it now.

For example, I hate snakes. Or, more accurately, I hate the idea of snakes. I know that I could use cathartic processing to deal with my aversion to snakes, but my gut tells me not to for now. I know it wouldn't be too painful or distressing. I know exactly how I would do it. I would use an imaginary scene. (Warning: if you also have an aversion to snakes you might want to skip to the next paragraph.) In my imagination, I would be stranded on an island infested with all kinds of snakes. There would be plenty of fruit in the trees, but these trees would also be full of snakes. I wouldn't be able to catch enough fish to survive. My best alternative source of protein would be the snakes, so I'd have to find a way to deal with them. In my imagination, I would study them and think of how to deal with them until I had a catharsis. Someday, I will probably carry out this exercise--but right now, for whatever reason, I just don't want to.

Even though cathartic techniques are easy, you need to practice them. It's like physical exercise. You only benefit from physical exercise or cathartic processes if you practice them. It's something you do much more than something you know.

Let's say your body is very out of shape. You haven't exercised in years but you want to. You start jogging one block every other day for a week. The next week you jog two blocks every other day, and so on. In twenty weeks or so (depending on the distance of a block), you'd be running a mile. In ten years, you'd be running a twenty-six mile marathon. Your progress would be so gradual that you would feel little or no pain.

You can do something similar with the cathartic techniques. You can always focus on sensations that are pleasurable. Gradually you'll stumble onto subjects that are slightly painful. You could easily gain confidence and want to dive into experience that is very painful. After a while, you'll become clearer about what is best for you.

The techniques are also easy in that they don't usually include an effort to relax physical tension. Focusing attention on sensations naturally causes comfort and relaxes unnecessary tension. When you've focused enough attention on bodily sensations for long enough, your sensations will spontaneously relax, become comfortable, and start to assimilate.

THE AUTONOMIC NERVOUS SYSTEM, YOUR INNER LIZARD AND INNER DOG

Here are some theories, working definitions, and viewpoints about the autonomic nervous system and the triune brain. They are intended as helpful viewpoints that can make using the cathartic techniques easier.

The autonomic nervous system consists of the sympathetic nervous system and the parasympathetic nervous system. The sympathetic nervous system includes:

- arousal
- the fight-or-flight response
- increased heart rate
- increased blood flow to skeletal muscles (by as much as 1,200 percent) and the lungs
- increased metabolic rate
- dilation of the pupils and relaxation of the lens to allow more light to enter the eye
- constriction of blood vessels supplying the skin
- dilation of blood vessels supplying the heart.

In other words, you're ready for anything.

The parasympathetic nervous system is basically the opposite. It's involved with relaxation and rejuvenation. Think of having a big lunch, then lying in a hammock on a pleasant summer day. Your blood pressure decreases, your heart beats slower, and your digestion becomes more active.

Anxiety usually stimulates the sympathetic nervous system. It puts you on alert whether you need to be or not. If your mind perceives a threat, real or not, your body still reacts. A cat is perfectly calm and relaxed most of the time, or at least it seems. If it senses a threat, it will become alert and deal with the threat as best as it can. When the threat passes, it returns to its calm and relaxed state. It doesn't replay the event over and over in its mind. It doesn't get anxious about it. It doesn't build a neurosis around it.

THE REPTILIAN AND MAMMALIAN MINDS

The reptilian and mammalian minds are two parts of the triune brain theory. It's not necessarily scientific fact (parts are), but I think it's a very useful theory. More important, I think most people would agree that we have reptilian like impulses and behavior, and mammalian impulses and behavior.

The reptilian brain consists of the brainstem and cerebellum. The mammalian brain consists of the limbic system. It sits on top of and wraps around the reptilian brain. The neocortex handles conscious thought and language. The neocortex sits on top of and wraps around the mammalian brain.

The reptilian brain reacts before the mammalian brain reacts. The mammalian brain reacts before the neocortex reacts. That is why when you're startled, you can physically jump, then experience an emotional reaction such as fear or anger--all before you are consciously aware of those reactions.

THE REPTILIAN MIND

The basic characteristics of the reptilian mind are fight, flight, and fright. If you operated only with your reptilian mind, when you felt hungry you would search for food. You might go into a grocery store and start eating anything on the shelves. The store manager would approach you to ask what you were doing. If the store manager was very big and looked mean, you might freeze hoping that he won't see you. If that didn't work, you would probably run away. If the store manager looked meek, you might attack until the manager ran away; then you would continue eating. If the store manager started beating you before you could get

162

away, you would go into fright mode. You would physically freeze and lose consciousness.

Here's a personal example of how the reptilian mind operates. Several years ago, I lived in a house that had snakes in the backyard. They were about four feet long and I believe they were copperheads, which are poisonous. I saw them a few times when I mowed the yard. They were about ten feet away from me and didn't seem to care about me. Once, while on the first pass with the lawn mower, I looked to my right to see a snake reared up with its mouth open and charging at me. The next thing I new, I was on the other side of the yard. I must have jumped like a gazelle, but the snake was still charging. I jumped again, and then ran to the back steps where I felt safe. The lawn mower was electric and plugged in near the snake's nest. That lawn mower ran for about a half hour until I got the nerve to go unplug it.

My reptilian brain made me jump, thankfully, before my conscious mind knew what had happened. My reptilian brain didn't wait for me to consciously decide anything about the snake and that was very good.

However, after that experience, every time I saw something in my peripheral vision with the shape of a snake, it startled me. At first, my reaction was so strong that it startled people around me. This was a problem. I resisted feeling startled and that added anxiety on top of it. Back then, I didn't know about trying to achieve a catharsis, but I did try to relive the experience in my mind so I could be more comfortable with it.

Soon after that, I had a dream about a big snake in my backyard. It slowly approached me and bit me although it was a playful friendly bite as a dog might do. I must have achieved something of a catharsis from that dream. After that I thought--and more important, I felt--that the real snake was just being a snake. Maybe it had babies and was only protecting them. It didn't bite me. Maybe it didn't really want to. When something startled me that only looked like a snake, I no longer added anxiety on top of feeling startled. My startle response began to fade away and after a few weeks was gone.

That is an example of how the reptilian mind reacts, how it remembers, and how catharsis restores equilibrium. My neocortex, that is, my conscious thinking mind, wasn't part of or a help with my response to the attack. Afterward, my wishing that I didn't feel startled created anxiety on top of feeling startled. It took a dream to help me begin to unite my thinking mind with my primitive or reactive mind.

The Reptilian Mind's Fight-or-Flight Response

Experiences that trigger the fight-or-flight response are usually unpleasant, so resistance and blocking memes can easily be part of remembering the event. If a dog suddenly attacked and bit you, you would react instantly with the fight-or-flight response. If strong resistance to that memory habituated, you could feel the fight-or-flight response whenever you see any dog. Resistance or diversion stops further conscious processing of the memory. You wouldn't remember any details about the attack, and you wouldn't think about the attack in more detail. Because of that, whenever you see another dog, you remember or associate the dog that attacked you. You remember, and relive, only the fight-or-flight response. Without processing the memory in more detail, the fight-or-flight response is the full memory and all there is to remember. Since the fight-or-flight response happens automatically, it's easy to think it's not part of you. You try to dissociate from the response and resist it.

If you had little or no resistance to the memory of the dog that attacked you, you could see that you just happened to walk within a foot of the dog. The dog had newborn puppies and reacted defensively as dogs might when they have puppies. You looked at the dog and sensed that it was upset. The owner of the dog assures you that it has never bitten anyone before. You sense that is true so you don't demand the owner have the dog destroyed. With that much clarity, you have a catharsis. You add awareness to the experience beyond just the fight-or-flight response. You don't react with fear every time you see any dog. You spent time perceiving the situation and thinking about it in more detail. With every new detail you add to the experience, the fight-or-flight response is no longer needed and fades away.

Possibly, even the dog that attacked you also had a catharsis. It watched while its owner talked to you and shook your hand. The dog saw its owner's relief when you decided not to have the dog destroyed. Now the dog is likely to lick you.

But What Is the Fight, Flight, or Fright Response?

For catharsis and the cathartic techniques, I don't think a detailed discussion about fight, flight, or fright is needed. Everyone seems to have a useful understanding of those responses, even if they aren't exactly the same between any two people. Assimilation, and its awareness, will dissolve or resolve any of those reactions equally. However, the fly-on-the-wall technique (page 68), probably works best for dealing with habituated fright or freezing.

THE MAMMALIAN MIND

Some basic characteristics of the mammalian mind--your inner dog--are a sense of love, a sense of belonging to a group, tribe or community; feeling liked and accepted by others; feeling rejected by others; being a leader or follower of others; joy, loneliness, jealousy, grief, and so on.

If you operated with only your mammalian mind (and your reptilian mind because all mammals also have a reptilian mind), you would search for food when you felt hungry. You would go into a grocery store and start eating. If you saw a friend, you might eat together, groom each other or play with your food. You might offer your food to your friend. If you saw a group of people that you belonged to, perhaps your family, you would eat with them. When the store manager started yelling at your friend or a member of your family, you would get very angry and try to protect that person. The entire group would attack the manager. Depending on how many police officers arrived, your group would either stand and fight, or scatter and run away. The next time you went to that store, you would try to avoid the manager.

Emotion

I think it's clear that no one really knows exactly what emotions are, or what causes them. If the following prompts you to come up with a different definition that is more helpful to you, then that would be ideal.

An emotion is an interpretation or evaluation of experience. It's a sense and a reaction that come from your mammalian mind. Like the reptilian mind, the mammalian mind has only two basic senses: threat or validation. The reptilian mind senses physical threat or physical validation. The mammalian mind, via emotion, senses social threat, or social validation. It senses whether a person or a group of people accepts you or not. It senses others' anger, aggression, rejection, affection, admiration, and so on. It responds with rage, passion, joy, sadness, resignation (depression), and so on.

Either sensory perception or a thought can produce an emotional response. If John looked at you with an angry, aggressive expression, your emotional response would arise from your senses. If a third person told you that John hated you, you could have the same emotional response even though John is friendly toward you. Your emotions don't distinguish between a perceived threat and an imagined one.

Between your senses and thoughts, things can move very fast and get very complicated. The interaction between your senses and thoughts can move so fast that's it hard to tell what caused a particular emotion.

For example, John seems friendly to you, but he doesn't look you in the eye very much, so you're afraid of him. You knew someone who behaved the same way in the past, and they were mean to you. Mary told you that John hates you. Mary was interested in John, but John rejected her. Bob told you John is a nice guy. You trust Bob, but you're interested in Mary. Your attraction to Mary influences you more than your trust in Bob. You become convinced that John is out to get you, and you angrily confront him. John becomes confused, upset, and almost cries. Now you sense John doesn't dislike you at all and you feel like a complete idiot.

In that scenario, all the emotions arising from your senses and your thoughts could have happened in a fraction of a second. In that scenario, there were only two emotions that you sensed: John seemed friendly; John is emotionally hurt and almost cries. Your other emotions, fear and anger, were based on ideas that others told you or memories outside your experience with John. Your attraction to Mary and your trust in Bob might arise from your senses, but they weren't directly from your experience with John. If your emotions were fully assimilated during that scenario, you would be more able to evaluate your experiences, see them as options, and choose to react to them or not.

Just like conscious, higher-brain thought, an emotion is valid or true only if you judge it to be valid or true. Sometimes an emotion is more useful and accurate than a thought, and sometimes a rational thought is more useful and accurate than emotion. Emotions are almost constantly active, just as your conscious (or subconscious) internal dialogue can ramble on all day. You don't respond to or use most of your emotions any more than you respond to most of your thoughts or internal dialogue that pass through your mind.

Your mind can become fixated on a perceived threat or an emotion, causing persistent overstimulation of the sympathetic nervous system. That overstimulation can cause anxiety or depression.

When is a reptilian or mammalian impulse appropriate or useful? When is an emotion appropriate? That's for your judgment, and maybe your soul, to decide. In my experience and in general, my emotions are frequently much smarter than my "higher" conscious rational mind. For example, I don't drive a car often, but when I do, I am usually nervous and afraid during the first five minutes. I interpret that as my emotions telling me that I need to be more attentive. My emotions are usually correct. When I first start driving, I usually look around too much.

On the other hand, sometimes I get nothing from focusing on an emotion. I try to give all my emotions as much attention as I can, but I'm not surprised if doing that doesn't seem to go anywhere. Sometimes an emotion that seemed stupid to me comes back a week later with a juicy revelation sitting on top of it.

THE THINKING MIND

Your thinking mind allows you to understand such concepts as a civilized society. You can understand that taking your groceries to the cashier and paying for them is part of being in a civilized society. You can understand that having a job is part of a civilized society. You can understand that civilization can (or should) make survival easier and less conflicted. You might tell the store manager that you think the prices are too high or that you would like the store to stock a particular product.

HOW THE REPTILIAN, MAMMALIAN, AND THINKING MINDS INTERACT AND AFFECT EACH OTHER

Let's speculate about the characteristics of each of theses minds, how they interact, and how they affect each other.

The reptilian mind doesn't know the past, present or future. It knows only what is happening in the moment. It deals only with what can be seen, heard, or physically felt. It's not capable of abstract thought, such as 2 + 2 = 4. It can sense hunger and has a drive to survive. It can sense danger and react by fighting or running away.

The reptilian mind sees the thinking and mammalian mind as external to itself. It doesn't know the difference between a growling dog in your thoughts and a real growling dog. The reptilian mind doesn't react nearly as much to a growling dog in your thoughts, because there isn't nearly as much sensory detail. The more you clearly imagine, in detail, a growling dog three feet from you, the more you'll feel a sympathetic nervous system response. Also, you can willfully repress your reaction to anything you think about because you're consciously aware that you're only thinking.

The mammalian mind can sense care and concern from others; it can be caring and concerned for others. It desires concern from others and wants to care for others. It can sense positive regard or aggression. It's political. It understands group dynamics. It can make decisions about how to affect group dynamics. It can sense its role in the group. The mammalian mind can sense short periods of time. It senses loss of affection from others. It can anticipate what others will do and act accordingly. Most emotion comes from the mammalian mind.

The reptilian mind will react to mammalian senses. The fight-or-flight response will activate when someone makes fun of you. When someone compliments you, the reptilian mind can react as if you'd just found an easy and delicious meal.

The thinking mind can understand simple or complex abstractions such as 2 + 2 = 4, or the nature and interactions of atoms. Its sense of time and space has no limits.

If the content of your thoughts primarily involves the senses, the primitive mind will react. The primitive mind doesn't process abstract thought. If the content is social, the mammalian emotional mind will react.

The thinking mind can resist the reptilian and mammalian minds. The reptilian and mammalian minds can at least seem to fight back against this resistance. Possibly, they don't fight back at all. The attempt to resist them causes anxiety for as long as a reptilian or mammalian impulse is active--although resisting an impulse can cause it to be active indefinitely.

The thinking mind constantly generates ideas and definitions of resisted experience, and why the experience keeps happening. The ideas tend to be inaccurate because awareness of detail in resisted experience is low. That lack of detail generates delusional ideas. Because you base your reactions on inaccurate ideas, your reactions are neurotic. If you fully accept an experience, you won't feel a need to ponder it unless you see it relates to something that is currently happening.

HIGHEST MIND

What follows is certainly a matter of opinion, but it's good to ponder. Here are my ponderings.

If you are operating at the level of your highest mind, your assessment of your situation, in the moment and in general, is realistic and accurate. You're clear about what you know and what you don't know. If there are no real threats, you don't feel threatened or anxious and you don't react defensively. You have no anxiety or inner conflict. Your level of stimulation is appropriate for your environment and situation. You accept all emotions as useful input. All impulses are considered and never resisted. You can ponder existence, God, and the best and fairest form of government. You clearly see a difference between fact and your experience. You can fully and objectively express your experience to anyone who is interested, and you enjoy listening to anyone do the same.

CPSIA information can be obtained at www.ICGtesting.com
Printed in the USA
BVOW011209100313

315125BV00010B/141/P